RELEASE

YOUR

WORRIES

A guide to letting go of stress and anxiety

CATE HOWELL AND
MICHELE MURPHY

ROBINSON • LONDON

Constable & Robinson Ltd
55–56 Russell Square,
London WC13 4HP
www.constablerobinson.com

First published in Australia in 2011 by Exisle Publishing

First published in the UK by Robinson,
an imprint of Constable & Robinson Ltd, 2011

A copy of the British Library Cataloguing in
Publication data is available from the British Library

Important

This book is not intended as a substitute for advice or medical treatment.
Any person with a condition requiring medical attention should consult a
qualified medical practitioner or suitable therapist.

ISBN: 978-1-78033-117-1

Printed and bound in the EU

CONTENTS

INTRODUCTION

*Happiness is not a state to arrive at,
rather, a manner of travelling.*

—Samuel Johnson (1709–84)

This book is about stress and anxiety and what helps to manage them. This is not another complicated textbook – it has been written to meet the need for a readable, understandable and enjoyable book on stress and anxiety. It is based on our 50+ combined years of experience working with people with stress or anxiety in individual, group therapy and teaching situations. Our experience combines medical and psychological knowledge as well as a holistic approach to health. Consequently, we believe this book will be invaluable to individuals experiencing stress or anxiety, their friends and families, and a range of health or other students and professionals.

Stress and anxiety are common. Almost one-fifth of individuals will experience significant anxiety in their lifetime. *Release Your Worries* was written to give you hope that things can be different and so you don't have to feel that stress and anxiety are running your life. You are definitely not alone – in fact, you may be surprised to know that many successful people throughout history, including Winston Churchill and

Oprah Winfrey, have experienced anxiety and panic. This book contains stories based on real situations, to help highlight ideas that we have found useful.

This book will provide a range of reliable and up-to-date strategies to put you back in the driver's seat of your life. It will be useful at any stage of your journey with stress or anxiety – especially at the beginning of the journey when information is crucial to help you understand what is happening and what you can do about it, during the journey to help guide you as to what approaches suit you as an individual and also at the end, to look back on, and celebrate, your progress.

We use a 'multimodal' approach to the management of stress and anxiety, drawing on many different models of therapy, because we believe one size does not fit all. Please don't worry if you find some of the ideas do not suit you; we aim to present a wide range of strategies, so that some of them will fit you and your life.

We also believe that each person is a unique individual. Your knowledge of yourself will guide you to choose the strategies that are going to be most helpful to your particular needs, and we encourage you to use your expert knowledge on what will be helpful to you. Our thinking is that the strategies in this book will help you to identify the strengths and resources you already have and help you build on them.

In this book, we will challenge many taken-for-granted ways of being and thinking that may be blocking you from being the person you want to be or may be pushing you to act in ways that are uncharacteristic. We will guide you towards ideas and strategies that will enable you to reach your potential in health and enjoyment of life. The great news is that these strategies and skills will be yours to use long after the original problem of stress or anxiety has gone. Hence, you will have the confidence of knowing you have a range of experience and skills that you can use to face future challenges in life.

This guide will help you:

- identify the signs and symptoms of stress and anxiety
- manage the symptoms of stress and anxiety
- develop a range of strategies and skills to help prevent and manage possible future challenges in your life
- gain an understanding or world-view that may help you enjoy your life more fully.

About this journey

This book has been developed to enable you to change the parts of your life that need to be changed, in order to facilitate your own journey towards managing stress and anxiety. We believe it will also assist you in gaining a greater sense of compassion towards yourself and your wellbeing. We have chosen the metaphor of a journey to convey the information we wish to share, because we have found this a useful way for people to visualise, understand and contemplate making changes in their lives. We have addressed different issues in each chapter of this book as a way of providing a potential 'map' of your own journey to managing the stress and anxiety that has been pushing you around.

You may feel that stress or anxiety is blocking you from living the kind of life you would prefer. You may even believe that the thought of addressing the stress or anxiety is as daunting as climbing Mount Everest – you may feel ill-equipped and fearful of what lies ahead. In the past you may have tried different strategies to address the anxiety but they did not work. Perhaps you embarked on your climb up your personal stress or anxiety mountain with bare feet, no water and having not exercised in years! In other words, you set yourself up for failure. However, if you had been provided with a 'travel kit' of things to make your journey easier, had engaged in some training or practice to increase stamina and confidence, and had also become aware of your own personal resources, the journey would have had a much greater chance of success. This book will provide you with the travel kit for your own successful personal journey.

We will introduce concepts, and return to them when relevant later in the book. Sometimes we repeat ideas because they are important, or we might want to expand on them later on. At the end of each chapter there will be a summary of important points called 'Travel reminders'. They can be photocopied and placed in your purse or wallet, or magnetised to put on the fridge or placed anywhere you feel will be the most helpful to your progress. There are also 'Travel diary' pages at the end of each chapter, to enable you to jot down points from the chapter which you find particularly helpful, to record your progress or to write down questions to ask your doctor or therapist. We hope you find this book respectful, useful, 'down to earth' and enjoyable.

Your journey may take many different forms. At times it may feel like a mountain climb, a bus ride, a car trip or perhaps a leisurely stroll in the park. Dr Russ Harris, in his book *The Happiness Trap*, has suggested that working through a book can be like a journey into a foreign country where much seems strange and new. At times the new country can be exciting and exhilarating, but at the same time a bit frightening or challenging. Sometimes you will think that the new country is better than the old country. However, when you are tired it may feel easier to stay in the old country, because it is familiar and takes less effort to manage.[1]

We are in no sense experts on your own particular journey. It is as if we are travel guides who have had the privilege of travelling many different journeys with many different people. All of these journeys were unique, but because we have experienced so many we have been able to draw out some similarities or signposts to the journeys that were most helpful in relieving stress and anxiety. It is in no way that we are better, less anxious, smarter, or stronger than you. It is just a matter of distance and perspective.

In fact, even though we have gained a lot of specialist knowledge through years of formal study, our most precious lessons and insights have come from fellow travellers with whom we have had the honour of working over the years. This is another reason we emphasise the importance of your expert knowledge about your own journey. Although this book may open up many different directions for you, ultimately you are responsible for choosing your own way and putting in the effort it will take to complete that journey.

The good news is that there is hope and help for your journey. Your brain is both complex and amazing, and through knowledge, strategies and practice, it can learn new ways of being. This guide will provide some of the knowledge and strategies, and encourage you to put them into practice. So, let's get started on the journey.

CAUTION

We think it is very important to put a 'warning' label on this book, as we have seen some clients who have felt worse after reading a 'self-help' book! This might have been because they believed that the book would 'fix' the problem, or that they did not 'measure up' in relation to the messages in the book. The aim of our book is to assist and encourage you. You will find we express a number of times in the book that we believe you are the expert on you. As a result, we urge you to choose the ideas that suit you from the book, and to ignore the others that do not fit with your expert knowledge of yourself.

What we are really saying is that we would be mortified if this book was used as a means of 'self-destruction'. We would not want your mind to 'whip' you for 'not reading the book', 'not following the book', 'not measuring up to what the book says'. If this is difficult for you to do, you may like to work through the book with a therapist or see a therapist alongside working through the book yourself. Our care instructions for you (not the book!) are quite clear: this book is to be read with self-compassion and self-kindness ever present and with the express goal of guiding you towards things that make your life better for you, not worse.

ALL ABOUT STRESS AND ANXIETY

Not until we are lost do we begin to understand ourselves.

—Henry Thoreau (1817–62)

All individuals experience stress in their life journey, whether stress occurs at work, on social occasions or at home. A degree of stress can be 'a friend', as it may help us to function well, but too much stress may interfere with our life.[1] This is especially so in today's world as we live in complex times, and lead busy and demanding lives. An individual may also have high expectations of themselves and all aspects of their life (personal, emotional, social, spiritual, occupational and financial), and become stressed when they perceive that they are not reaching these expectations.

As you will read later in this chapter, humans are designed to respond to sudden or acute, short-term stress, but a lot of today's stresses are ongoing, such as family or financial worries. We are not so well equipped to cope with this chronic stress. Stress can be helpful and spur us on to achieve things, but unfortunately stress can also impact on our quality of life and health. When we are stressed, we might turn for relief to certain foods or activities, such as drinking too much alcohol or working late, and these behaviours can have a negative impact on our health and wellbeing. This guide will help you understand your stress triggers and how you react to stress, so that you can find different ways to manage it.

Anxiety is also a normal and universal emotion, and is related to one of the key human emotions: fear. We all know the feeling of fear, whether experiencing fear related to a job interview, giving a talk or heights. We can recognise when we are feeling frightened or anxious by what we experience in our mind and body. These responses can help us survive in a dangerous situation, but in many cases anxiety can be distressing and can significantly interfere with a person's home life, relationships or work. The individual can feel demoralised, lose confidence, and their sense of self-esteem can be affected. Some people experience acute or sudden anxiety, while others might experience ongoing anxiety.

For all of these reasons, it is important to understand the nature of stress and anxiety, and to learn ways to reduce them both. This chapter will focus on 'psycho-education' or providing information on the nature of stress and anxiety, including what causes them and how to recognise them. Some of the common myths about anxiety and the impact of stress and anxiety on health will be highlighted, and you will be introduced to the range of strategies which can be learnt and practised, and which will help you let go of stress and anxiety.

There is more and more evidence that the brain is capable of reorganising itself as you learn and practise. There are billions of interconnecting nerve cells in the brain. In the past, the brain was thought to be rigid in structure. Current thinking, however, is that the brain has the ability to change in response to experience; this is called 'neuroplasticity'.[2] Whenever you learn something new, including a skill or strategy related to managing stress and anxiety, the brain changes. New neuronal (nerve cell) connections or 'wiring' form, so that in the future you will be more relaxed.[3] These new neuronal connections are strengthened through repetition and practice. This is why we recommend that, as you read this book, you practise the strategies a number of times. Throughout the book we have also repeated important ideas and strategies, because we believe this repetition will also assist in reinforcing new pathways.

It is also important to remember that you are an individual, and that you will take different things from this guide than another person, but that is what we want – we will present a whole lot of information, ideas and strategies and from this you can take what suits you. We will pose different questions and tasks for you to work through. There are no right or wrong answers; the tasks are included to help you understand your unique, individual self and to stimulate your thoughts and ideas.

The good news message from this book is that stress and anxiety can be managed in different ways and reduced, and you can develop a greater sense of peace and wellbeing as a result. Remember that you are not alone, and that there is help available. Many individuals have overcome stress or anxiety by using resources such as this guide and seeking support or professional help if need be.

The place to begin this journey of understanding stress and anxiety, and managing the associated symptoms and their impact, is by looking at some definitions.

Stress

Stress is defined as a response to a demand which we are experiencing, such as responding to a hungry child, dealing with a problem at work or making a decision. However, stress is an individual experience, and has different meanings to different people. Some people might describe stress as tension, others as worry, or feeling overwhelmed or out of control.[4]

The quotes below highlight the different ways in which different individuals experience stress.

> *When I feel out of control and unable to fix the problem, or when it is unfixable. Then it feels overwhelming.*
>
> —Sue

> *I feel stressed when I have everyone wanting something from me, my boss, my girlfriend and my parents. Just too many things all at once. I wish they would leave me alone.*
>
> —John

NOW CONSIDER THE FOLLOWING:
What does stress mean to you?
How would you define stress?

_____

_____

_____

_____

_____

Fear

Fear is a normal human response to a danger or threat, whether it is real or imagined. It is a reaction to what is or could be happening in the moment.[5] Most people feel scared or worry about some things, such as a child being afraid of the dark or of dogs, or adults having a degree of fear about flying. However, some worries or fears are bigger than others, and sometimes a person might need help in dealing with them.

Anxiety

Anxiety is part of life and everyone experiences it. It is one of the emotions we are born with, and it is generally an unpleasant one. There are some similarities between excitement and anxiety, and it is a lot like fear. However, anxiety is typically about something that might happen in the future.[6] When a person feels anxious, they might be anticipating a problem or there might actually be some element of danger, such as when driving on a busy motorway. Anxiety is often described as a feeling of impending danger.[7]

However, when anxiety is excessive or interferes with the person's ability to lead their life, such as their ability to work or to go to social functions, it becomes a problem. Some individuals feel constantly anxious or they may experience episodes of extreme fear or panic, commonly called a 'panic attack' or 'episode'.[8] When anxiety symptoms are distressing and interfere with the person's ability to carry out their daily activities, the degree of anxiety is significant and is referred to as an anxiety disorder. Types of anxiety disorders include generalised anxiety disorder, social anxiety disorder, panic disorder, obsessive-compulsive disorder and post-traumatic stress disorder. These terms will be explained in more detail later in this chapter.

The following two examples start to show how anxiety can significantly impact on an individual's life:

> *Anxiety is when I worry constantly about something or many things, and I can't stop thinking about it, I can't sleep, and it makes everything else seem worse. It brings me down.*
>
> —Bill

> *Anxiety comes on quickly, starting with a feeling in my stomach, then my heart races, and I just want to be swallowed up into the ground and disappear, so I don't have to feel it.*
>
> —Sarah

OTHER EXAMPLES OF FEARS AND ANXIETIES

- Mary is confident in her work, but becomes very anxious at work social functions.
- John has a fabulous new apartment, but if there is a spider in the apartment, John is out of it.
- Lou had a panic attack at the local shopping centre, and now dreads going there. He avoids it whenever he can.
- Ashley works as a nurse, but worries that she will make a mistake and harm a patient. As a result she constantly checks patient wristbands and notes to make sure she does not make a mistake when giving out medications. She is spending so much time checking that her manager has called her in for a meeting.

ANXIETY IS UNIVERSAL

Significant anxiety is one of the most common mental health problems in communities across the globe. Researchers have gathered results from studies of anxiety from the United States of America, Europe, the Middle East, Canada, Asia, South America and New Zealand. They have found that in the general population, the one-year prevalence rate of anxiety is 10.6 per cent; that is, 10.6 per cent of people will experience anxiety over a 12-month period.[9] A recent survey of Australian adults found a prevalence rate of 14.4 per cent, with women experiencing higher rates than men (18 per cent versus 11 per cent).[10]

The lifetime prevalence rate of anxiety is reported to be 16.6 per cent, which means that almost 17 per cent of individuals will experience significant anxiety in their lifetime.[11] This is almost one-fifth of individuals. Importantly, most adults with anxiety disorders do not receive appropriate treatment, with only 5.1 per cent receiving psychological treatment and 3.8 per cent being prescribed appropriate medication.[12] This is why guides such as this are useful and important, to provide information on anxiety and its treatment, strategies for managing anxiety, and advice on how to access extra assistance when needed.

ANXIETY AND DEPRESSION

It is also important to be aware that anxiety may co-exist with depression. Depression is characterised by persistent depressed mood and/or loss of pleasure or interest in almost all activities. There is a range of other symptoms such as: low energy, poor sleep or concentration, changed eating patterns or thoughts of worthlessness or guilt.[13] It has been established that stressful life events are likely to play a role in the onset or relapse of depression. Loss and grief may also be a trigger. It is important to determine whether depression is also present alongside anxiety to make sure the most appropriate help is sought and provided.

How the body and mind react to stress

When an individual is under stress, their mind and body will react. These responses are adaptive – that is, they help us to survive. The stress response is designed to protect us and not harm us. In the age of the 'caveman', an everyday danger would have been coming face to face with a dangerous animal, such as a sabre-toothed tiger, when out hunting for food. The caveman would have been fearful of the tiger, which would have been able to kill him in an instant.

In this scenario, the caveman would have seen the tiger in his path, recognised the danger, and then a number of changes would have automatically happened in his body and mind. These changes (shown in figure 1 on page 15) would have included:

- A change in blood flow to prepare the body for activity. There would have been a redirection of blood flow from the brain, skin and extremities (fingers, toes), the intestines and other organs to the muscles, so that the caveman could either run away or fight the tiger. These changes would also mean that if the tiger cut the caveman on the limbs, he would have been less likely to bleed to death.
- The movement of glucose from stores in the body into the blood to provide energy to run or fight.
- An increase in alertness through the senses (hearing, sight, smell) to enable the caveman to accurately see and hear what the tiger was doing or preparing to do. The pupils would have enlarged in response.

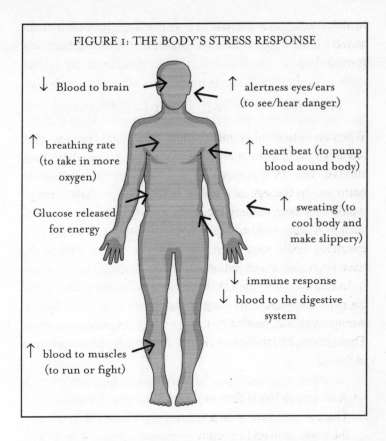

FIGURE 1: THE BODY'S STRESS RESPONSE

↓ Blood to brain

↑ alertness eyes/ears
(to see/hear danger)

↑ breathing rate
(to take in more
oxygen)

↑ heart beat (to pump
blood aound body)

Glucose released
for energy

↑ sweating (to
cool body and
make slippery)

↓ immune response
↓ blood to the digestive
system

↑ blood to muscles
(to run or fight)

- An increase in sweating to cool the body and make the skin slippery.
- A reduction in saliva production in the mouth.
- A reduction in other body functions, such as the immune system or digestion, as they were no longer the priority.[14]
- The heart rate increases to pump blood to necessary parts of the body.
- The breathing rate speeds up to take more oxygen into the body.

Today, the danger might not be a wild animal; instead, it might be job redundancy, a family conflict, a financial threat, or a divorce dispute. But the same reactions occur in our bodies today as they did in caveman times. That is because our bodies and minds are programmed to respond to danger by producing changes in the nervous and hormonal systems, known as the 'fight or flight response'.[15] The physical changes that accompany stress are intense but tend to be of limited duration, often no more than half an hour, and rarely beyond an hour. In fact, our bodies are not capable of keeping up these sorts of changes for long periods of time.[16]

The changes begin through the action of a number of structures in the body and brain. When we are in danger, the brain is generally stimulated causing an increased nervousness and alertness. The hypothalamus and pituitary gland in the brain are also stimulated and trigger an increase in activity in the sympathetic nervous system, which controls functions such as blood flow, heart rate, breathing rate, blood pressure and sweating.

The stress response also activates the adrenal glands, which release a number of hormones into the blood stream (adrenaline, noradrenaline and cortisol). These hormones also increase the sympathetic nervous system effects. That is why we might experience a racing heart or palpitations when we are stressed or anxious, rapid breathing, sweating or feeling hyper-alert. It is also why it takes time for the stress feelings and nervousness to settle, as it takes a while for the hormones to dissipate and slowly decrease to nothing.

WHY ME AND WHY NOW?
One of the first questions clients often ask about stress and anxiety is, 'Why am I experiencing it, and why now?' Sometimes there are very clear external factors or stressors,

such as pending examinations, a recent job loss or a marriage breakdown. Feelings of stress can be triggered by injury or illness, losing a relationship or a loved one through death. Often there is a series of stressors impacting on the individual, or several occurring together. But sometimes the reasons for the stress or anxiety are less obvious.

What are some of the triggers or stressors in your life that often result in stress (for example, a difficult boss or tricky teenager, or health or money worries)?

_____

_____

_____

_____

_____

The experience of stress is also influenced by 'internal' factors – how an individual responds to stress will be determined by their:

- perception of the stress (some people might be threatened by going for a job interview, others might find it an invigorating challenge)
- personality factors (further information is provided below)
- expectations of themselves, especially if there are high expectations of doing well in a particular circumstance
- coping skills, or skills learnt in the past to help cope with stress.
- available support.[17]

There are several factors which may play a role in the development of anxiety. Firstly, some anxiety disorders are more common in first-degree relatives of sufferers; that is, there may be an inherited tendency to anxiety. Sometimes it is hard to work out how much of the anxiety is related to inheritance and how much is due to life experiences. The story below illustrates how anxiety may tend to be experienced by a number of family members.

CATHY'S STORY

Cathy found herself worrying as a child about her schoolwork and friends. At night, she would go over and over the events of the day, and she would worry about what had happened and what had been said. To get to sleep, she would tell herself, 'Today is over, no point worrying – tomorrow is a new day.' At times this helped a lot.

Cathy's mother, Andrea, would worry too, about anything and everything. She especially worried about her health. Cathy's grandfather had been the same, and had also suffered from depression as a young man.

SYMPTOMS – PHYSICAL AND BEHAVIOURAL CAUSES

Some medical conditions (such as an overactive thyroid gland), and some medications can cause anxiety symptoms. The symptoms of severe anaemia, for example, may mimic anxiety symptoms. For this reason, if there is significant anxiety it is important to have a check-up with your GP to make sure any physical causes are identified and treated.[18]

There may be 'behavioural' causes of anxiety, in which the person's experiences in life may be associated with the development of specific fears, phobias or obsessions (persistent and intrusive thoughts).[19] For example, a child may develop a phobia of dogs after being chased by one, and then may learn to deal with this by avoiding areas where dogs might be. This is referred to as 'conditioning'.[20] The story below illustrates the influence of experience in the development of fears.

WILL'S STORY

Will was twenty months old when his mother, Sandy, noticed a lot of bees in the back garden, and dead bees on the ground. As toddlers tend to fall quite a lot, and roll around on the grass when playing, Sandy was concerned that Will might be stung. She had concerns that this would be painful, and was worried by the thought, 'What if Will is allergic to bees?' Also, Sandy was scared of bees as a young child herself.

As a result, whenever Sandy saw Will outside, she would point to the bees and say, 'Be careful, don't play there because there are bees. Ouch, hurt.' Very soon Will would point to the bees and say 'Ouch', and move towards his mother. He did not get stung, but became increasingly scared of bees. He would run away from a bee whenever he spotted one.

One day, Sandy spotted a lot of bees near the back shed, and found that there was a hive in the roof of the shed. Getting rid of the hive sorted out the problem with the bees, but Will remained scared of them for a number of years. When he was stung by a bee at seven years old, he said, 'It wasn't that bad', and his fear disappeared.

Personality is said to influence the development of anxiety, and some people have personality traits that may contribute to a tendency towards anxiety.[21] They may tend to be avoidant in behaviour, or be more obsessive about things than the next person. Being obsessive is not necessarily a bad thing (for example, it is helpful when doctors and nurses are obsessive in their care of a sick patient, or when musicians make sure they practise regularly), but when obsessiveness becomes excessive, it is a problem. An example of excessive obsessiveness was given earlier with the story of Ashley the nurse repeatedly checking patient wristbands out of fear of harming patients.

Other factors which may influence the development of anxiety are early life traumas, and difficult social and economic circumstances. As mentioned earlier in this chapter, anxiety disorders can also occur alongside other mental health problems such as depression.[22]

Recognising stress and anxiety

In this section we will look at some ways of recognising and measuring stress and anxiety. Let's look at stress to begin with.

STRESS
You will recognise many of the common symptoms and signs of stress, such as feeling tense, shaking, sweating, rapid breathing or a racing heart (palpitations), and you have also thought about how stress affects you. We have also highlighted that stress can be both a positive and negative experience for the individual.

It is also useful to think about how stress can produce physical signs, cognitive (thinking) signs, emotional and behavioural (changes in actions) signs. Table 1 outlines some of these signs. Are you aware of any others? If so, add them at the end of the table.

TABLE 1: SIGNS OF STRESS

Physical	**Cognitive**
Headaches	Negative thoughts
Indigestion	Thoughts about not being able
Heart palpitations	to cope, about 'losing
Muscle tension, twitches	control' or 'going crazy'
Muscle aches and pains	Loss of concentration
Fatigue	Impaired judgement or
Rashes	decision-making
Clenched jaw	Forgetfulness, mind going
Shortness of breath	blank
Dizziness	Bad dreams
Increased sweating	
Increased urination	
Constipation or diarrhoea	
Emotional	**Behavioural**
Nervousness	Eating more or less
Tension	Increased smoking or alcohol
Lack of enthusiasm, motivation	Increased coffee or energy
Loss of confidence	drinks
Decrease in pleasure in	Problems managing time
activities	Rushing things – having
A sense of unreality	mishaps, accidents,
Irritable, snappy	clumsiness
	Avoiding different situations

Think about a time when you have experienced severe stress (not necessarily the most severe, but still severe). Describe the situation and the symptoms you experienced.

_____

_____

_____

_____

_____

_____

_____

_____

Now we will look at a way of grading how much stress you are under at any time, by using a simple 0–10 scale. Ask yourself, how would you grade your level of stress right now on a scale of 0 to 10 (0 = no stress, 10 = the most stress you have ever experienced)?

0   1   2   3   4   5   6   7   8   9   1 0

The higher the score out of 10, the higher your level of stress at the moment. This scale is a useful way of identifying stress now, but also monitoring how you are going over time by repeating the scale from time to time.

ANXIETY

Now for anxiety!

Think about a time when you have experienced significant (but not the most severe) anxiety. What was happening at that time?

_____

_____

_____

_____

_____

_____

_____

Again, you can use a 10-point rating scale, and ask yourself, how would you grade your level of anxiety right now on a scale of 0 to 10 (0 = no anxiety, 10 = the most anxiety you have ever experienced)?

0   1   2   3   4   5   6   7   8   9   1 0

The higher the score out of 10, the higher your level of anxiety at the moment.

Another approach is to consider signs for anxiety. Consider the list overleaf and see if you recognise one or a number of signs. Tick the signs you recognise in yourself – you may find that you recognise a few or a large number of these warning signs.

TABLE 2: SIGNS OF ANXIETY

Sign	Sign
Feeling on edge much of the time	Fear of experiencing again the feelings of a past traumatic event
Constantly worried about a lot of things	Worrying a lot about your health
Feeling irritable	
Tense or nervous much of the time	Fear of dying, 'going crazy' or something bad happening
Avoiding people or social situations	Having thoughts that are hard to control
Trembling, tingling, light-headedness, dizzy spells, sweating, urinary frequency, diarrhoea	Fear of being in a place that you can't get out of, or that you can't get out of without embarrassment
Feeling panicky in some situations	Fear of germs or infection
Sleeping poorly, having difficulty falling asleep	Compulsively checking, counting or cleaning things
Having difficulty relaxing	Headaches, neck aches, chest pain, joint pain or nausea
Fear of making a fool of yourself socially, or of other people watching you or drawing attention to yourself	Fear of having a serious illness tha the doctor can't detect
	Tiredness or fatigue
Using alcohol or sedatives to calm down or to get to sleep	

Source: Ashfield, S. 2004, *Taking Care of Yourself and Your Family: A resource book for good mental health*, Mid North Health.

You may want to discuss the signs you recognise with your GP or mental health professional. Further information is also provided overleaf about the different types of anxiety disorders and how they can affect individuals.

Anxiety disorders

There are a number of specific anxiety disorders, and these include:

- generalised anxiety disorder
- panic disorder
- agoraphobia
- specific phobias
- social anxiety disorder
- obsessive-compulsive disorder
- adjustment disorder and post-traumatic stress disorder.[23]

The most common anxiety disorders are generalised anxiety disorder and specific phobias.[24]

Generalised anxiety disorder (GAD): the individual experiences excessive and persistent worry about a variety of general life issues, such as family, health, work or finances.

Panic disorder: the individual has recurring and unanticipated periods of intense fear or discomfort, which are followed by persistent concern about having further attacks, or worry about the implications of having the panic attacks, such as losing control, having a heart attack, vomiting or passing out, dying, or going 'crazy'. A panic attack may include a number of the symptoms listed in Table 3, and the symptoms may occur in a cascade (or in a series with one following the other). More information on panic attacks will be covered in later chapters.

TABLE 3: SYMPTOMS OF PANIC ATTACKS

- Palpitations (pounding heart or fast heart rate)
- Excessive perspiration, shakes and tremor
- Feeling breathless or as if you are choking
- Chest pain or tightness
- Nausea or abdominal symptoms
- Dizziness or feeling faint
- Feeling out of touch with reality or 'out of your body'
- Feeling out of control
- A feeling of impending doom
- Tingling or numbness (in the hands or feet, or around the mouth)
- Hot or cold flushes

Source: Mental Health Foundation of Australia, 1998.

Agoraphobia (may be associated with panic disorder, but not always): the individual is anxious about being in a situation in which it may be difficult to escape or which may be embarrassing. They may be anxious about being able to find help if they do something humiliating or show obvious anxiety symptoms. This anxiety usually leads to avoidance of the feared situations, such as crowded places, buses or shopping centres.

Social phobia: the individual is anxious about being scrutinised or negatively appraised by others, in case they do something embarrassing or show obvious anxiety symptoms. This anxiety usually leads to avoidance of the feared situations, such as eating or speaking in front of others, or going to social gatherings.

Specific phobia: the individual has an unrelenting and irrational fear of a specific object or situation, such as a fear of enclosed spaces (claustrophobia), or a fear related to an animal or heights. This fear usually leads to avoidance of the object or situation.

Obsessive-compulsive disorder (OCD): the individual may experience unpleasant, intrusive obsessional thoughts, ideas, images and impulses that they find difficult to control, such as concerns about contaminating or harming themself or their family. These obsessional thoughts often lead to seemingly uncontrollable repetitive or stereotyped behaviours, including hand-washing, checking or counting. These behaviours are performed on the basis of preventing the occurrence of the unlikely event or to reduce anxiety.

Adjustment disorder and post-traumatic stress disorder (PTSD): these disorders are seen as reactions to severe stress. They operate on a continuum, with a mild reaction to stress at one end, adjustment disorders in the middle, and PTSD at the severe end of the spectrum. Adjustment disorder involves severe anxiety in response to an acute illness or psychological stress (such as a relationship breakdown). PTSD involves the development of long-lasting anxiety following a traumatic event. It is characterised by images, dreams or flashbacks of the event and a range of other symptoms.[25]

Debunking anxiety myths and misinterpretations

You may have many misconceptions about anxiety, including that it leads to heart attacks, can cause insanity, can lead to fainting, and can cause a loss of control.[26] Let's debunk some of the myths and misinterpretations surrounding anxiety one by one.

IT IS REAL

Yes, anxiety is real and it is probably the most basic of all emotions. Not only is it experienced by all humans, but anxiety responses have been found in all species of animals right down to the sea slug. Anxiety experiences vary in their severity, from mild uneasiness to extreme terror and panic. They can also vary in their length from a brief, almost fleeting flash to a seemingly constant all-day experience.

IT IS NOT HARMFUL

While anxiety is an unpleasant sensation, and we would not ask for a bucket full of it, it is not in the least bit dangerous. As we have already defined, anxiety is a response to danger or threat. Immediate anxiety is termed the fight or flight response because all of its effects are aimed toward either fighting or fleeing the danger. The number one purpose for anxiety is to protect you, not harm you. Therefore, it does not make any sense for nature to develop a mechanism whose purpose is to protect you but, as it is protecting you, is actually harming you.

YOU ARE NOT GOING TO HAVE A HEART ATTACK

You may have misinterpreted the symptoms of the fight or flight response and believed you were dying of a heart attack. Breathlessness, chest pain as well as palpitations and fainting can occur in heart disease. However, in heart disease the symptoms are generally directly related to effort. The harder you exercise, the worse the symptoms. Also, the symptoms will usually go away fairly quickly with rest. Heart disease will almost always produce major electrical changes in the heart which are picked up by electrocardiograph (ECG).

This is very different to the symptoms associated with anxiety attacks. Anxiety attacks often occur at rest and seem to have a mind of their own. In anxiety attacks the only change which shows up on an ECG is a slight increase in heart rate. Like exercise, anxiety causes temporary increases in blood pressure, and exercise is good for the heart. There is only a problem when blood pressure is constantly too high.

YOU ARE NOT LOSING CONTROL
You may have had the belief that you were going to 'lose control' during an anxiety attack. You may have feared that you will either become totally paralysed and not be able to move, or that you will not know what you are doing and may run around wildly, yelling out obscenities and embarrassing yourself. Alternatively, you may not have really thought about how it would look if you actually 'lost control' but you just experienced an overwhelming feeling of 'impending doom'.

It is important to remember that the anxiety response:
- is there to keep you safe and there has never been a recorded case of someone 'going wild' during an anxiety attack
- is not aimed at hurting other people (who are not a threat)
- will not produce paralysis
- may make you feel somewhat confused, 'unreal' and distracted, but you are still able to think and function normally
- is often invisible to others around you. Just think of how often other people even notice that you are having an anxiety attack.

YOU ARE NOT GOING CRAZY
You may have wondered if the anxiety symptoms were a sign that you were 'losing it' or 'going crazy'. These terms are neither helpful nor meaningful. Unfortunately the symptoms of severe mental illnesses are sometimes colloquially referred

to as 'craziness', and when people think about mental illness they often think about conditions involving psychotic symptoms. Such symptoms include hallucinations (for example, hearing derogatory voices or seeing frightening visual hallucinations), or delusions, which are firmly held beliefs that are not true (for example, a belief about receiving messages from an inanimate object). It is important to understand that no amount of stress or anxiety will cause these symptoms, and these symptoms are very different from anxiety symptoms.

YOU ARE UNLIKELY TO FAINT

You may have been frightened about what might happen to you as a result of your anxiety symptoms. Perhaps you have shared the belief that your nerves might become exhausted and collapse, resulting in you fainting. Nerves are not like electrical wires and anxiety cannot wear out, damage or 'use up' nerves. Ask yourself, 'Have I ever fainted during an anxiety attack?'

Again, fear about fainting may come from a misunderstanding about what causes someone to faint. Fainting is caused by a drop in blood pressure; that is, when blood pressure is very low then fainting occurs. When you experience anxiety your blood pressure increases because your heart is beating faster. Therefore you are very unlikely to faint when you are anxious.[27]

The impact of stress and anxiety on how we function

There are a number of negative effects of stress and anxiety, and these occur especially when stress or anxiety is prolonged. The negative effects are summarised on the opposite page.

TABLE 4: NEGATIVE EFFECTS OF STRESS AND ANXIETY

Physical	Emotional	Behavioural	Social
Headaches	Irritability or anger	Changes in eating, smoking or alcohol use	Inability to fulfil social roles
Tiredness	Poor concentraion	Nail biting	Impact on relationships at home or work
Sleeping problems	Overly sensitive/ reactive	Lowered libido	
Muscle tightness or cramps	Anxiety or depression symptoms		
Palpitations			
Chest discomfort			

Source: Evans, B., Coman, G. and Burrows, G.D. 1998, *Your Guide to Understanding and Managing Stress*, Mental Health Foundation of Australia, Victoria.

Write down any of the negative effects which you have experienced.

_____

_____

_____

_____

_____

_____

The mind and body are closely related, so that anxiety also affects physical health. It has similar effects to those mentioned in the table above. Those affected will often say that anxiety is very tiring, and that it disturbs sleep and eating habits. The individual may try to manage the anxiety with alcohol or marijuana, and these substances can also have negative effects on health and wellbeing. Stress has also been shown to affect the immune system, which protects us against viral and bacterial infections. This is why stressed or anxious individuals may find that they are more prone to colds and flu.[28]

Travel tips

Just by deciding to read this book you have taken one of the most courageous steps you can take. You have recognised that stress or anxiety is the problem and you have decided to do something helpful about it. Following are some positive points to think about as you start your journey.

STRENGTH

You may have had the thought that you must be weak to be pushed around by stress or anxiety. Ironically, it is just the opposite. You have probably spent what seems like a lifetime 'being strong' for everyone else and doing what needs to be done. You have probably handled much more difficult situations than the one you are in now. So you may be asking, 'Why me? Why now?'

We are not absolutely sure why stress or anxiety has decided to visit you now, but we believe that they can have a cumulative effect over time. That is, stress or anxiety can build up and express themselves suddenly for no apparent (or easily identifiable) reason. In our experience, it is often 'strong' people who experience stress or anxiety because they are the ones who have difficulty saying 'no', looking after themselves before others and maintaining a balanced lifestyle.

WEAKNESS

We discourage the idea that stress or anxiety reflects weakness. We believe that individuals with stress or anxiety often have a great passion for life and a fear of life being cut short, or they may have high expectations of themselves and not want to let anyone down.

Remember too that stress and anxiety are neither good nor bad. Sometimes they work for you and sometimes they work against you. Chances are, if you are reading this book, stress or anxiety is working more against you at the moment. This book will help you get things back in balance.

PLANNING

All memorable journeys require a bit of planning to make them a success. Similarly you may need to think about how you plan to work through this book in a way that best suits you.

Do you need to pencil in some special times in your diary to read this book? Do you need to tell someone else so that they can encourage you to continue? Write down your ideas here.

_____

_____

_____

_____

_____

_____

Do you also need to list some of the issues that may block you from progressing through this book as you would like? (By being aware of them you may be able to make sure they don't get in the way.) Jot down the potential blocks in the space below.

_____

_____

_____

_____

_____

_____

GUIDE
We used the word 'guide' in the subtitle of this book because we hope it will be a useful guide for your journey. You may use it as your only guide or you may wish to get information from other sources, such as reputable websites.

GATHERING INFORMATION
There are lots of places to gather information that may help you. There are libraries, websites and books. You will find many useful references in the 'Further resources' section at the end of this book.

FAMILY AND FRIENDS
You may wish to share your progress through the book with family and friends whom you trust. You may like to ask them to read the parts of the book you are working on to facilitate their understanding of the changes they may be seeing in you. It is also very powerful to have an audience to your successes

as they will reinforce your progress. You may be surprised how supportive other people in your life can be.

Alternatively, if you have confided in someone who does not seem to understand what you are experiencing, or you have found them to be discouraging in some way, it is okay to minimise your contact with them for a short while. Or just talk about issues other than the anxiety when you do have contact.

TRAVEL JOURNAL
Another great way of marking your progress is to keep a journal or diary. This may be a separate, private notebook, or you might like to use the 'Travel diary' pages at the end of each chapter.

A travel diary can have a number of functions:

- It is a convenient, safe and cheap way to express your feelings and ideas.
- You don't have to worry about reactions or hurting anyone's feelings. Just make sure you keep it in a safe place and it's accessible only by you. It provides a wonderful record of signposts of your progress. You may be astounded to read how bad you felt before you started to make the changes suggested in this book.
- Finally, it provides a strong, concrete reminder of the strategies that have worked for you in the past, in your journey towards letting go of stress and anxiety. Hence, if you happen to experience a setback you can consult your diary to get back on the right track that will lead you once again towards your values and goals.

PAST STRATEGIES THAT HAVE WORKED
It may be useful to list the strategies that have worked for you in the past, before you started reading this book. You may be

surprised to realise how much you already know about pushing anxiety out of your life. We have mentioned previously that you do not have to persevere with strategies that do not fit with you or have not worked for you in the past. However, we have learnt from many people that sometimes strategies that have not worked in the past can be worth experimenting with. For example, the strategy may have been used incorrectly, or perhaps you have changed and what did not work in the past may be useful now.

You can make a list below of any strategies that you think might be worth revisiting.

_____

_____

_____

_____

_____

_____

_____

_____

_____

'BABY' STEPS

It is very important to go slowly and steadily through this book. We have found that the idea of taking small or 'baby' steps when starting your journey is very useful. We will discuss this more in Chapter 2.

BEING IN THE PRESENT

We have found that depression is often situated in the past: past hurts, past losses, decisions we regret. We cannot change the past and this can be very frustrating and demoralising. Conversely, we have found that anxiety is often about the future. For example, the 'what ifs': 'What if I can't meet the deadline? What if I can't pay the mortgage?' This type of thinking is unhelpful because you can't solve a problem that has not happened yet. It is impossible. You cannot travel across that bridge until you come to it. Therefore, it is helpful to try to keep yourself in the present moment, as the present is a place where you can make some helpful choices on how you would like to live your life. We will discuss this concept more in later chapters.

THERAPIST

You may wish to work through this guide with a psychologist, GP or other health professional of your choice. Your therapist will be a great resource to ask questions of, express your feelings and thoughts to, and to support and encourage your progress. A therapist may also help you keep yourself accountable to your goals. You may be worried that you will get distracted and not follow through on your wishes for your life. It is also useful to write down your questions as you work through this guide, so that your therapist can provide the help you need effectively and efficiently. Throughout this guide, we have used the word 'therapist' as a general term to refer to the professional with whom you may be consulting, whether that is a psychologist, medical practitioner, other mental health professional or counsellor.

THERAPIES

There are many psychological therapies available that have been found to be helpful with stress and anxiety, and our experience has been influenced by all of them. These therapies include: Multimodal Therapy, Motivational Interviewing (MI), Cognitive Behavioural Therapy (CBT), Narrative Therapy, Relaxation Therapy and Hypnotherapy, mindfulness-based approaches, Constructive Living, and Acceptance and Commitment Therapy (ACT). These therapies may be used in individual therapy (one on one), or in a group programme.

There are also natural therapies or medications which may be helpful, and your GP and naturopath can answer any questions on these. The range of available approaches will be discussed further in Chapter 2, and you will find that we have drawn a number of strategies from them to share with you in this guide.

HOLISTIC APPROACH

In this guide we take a holistic approach to dealing with anxiety and stress. We believe that by addressing your whole lifestyle, you can not only reduce your stress and anxiety, but you can also aim for a greater sense of health and wellness. Balanced and healthy lifestyles include: healthy eating, exercise, adequate sleep, quitting smoking, relaxation, fulfilling and supportive relationships, meaningful work and other interests, humour and laughter. By its very nature, a healthy and balanced lifestyle involves seeing your health and wellbeing as important and taking time for yourself to nurture body, mind and spirit.

Taking a holistic approach also relates to our choice of the different types of therapeutic approaches which may be of benefit. We utilise a number of different therapies, as they each have valuable approaches to stress and anxiety and skills to learn. Each individual is different and will relate to different approaches.

EFFORT

It makes sense that most skills take some effort to learn and get better with practice. An example is playing a musical instrument, or playing sport. The more you practise, the greater your sense of mastery and confidence in your new skills. Remember that 'work will – wishing won't'. The bottom line is that with a bit of effort you can reach your destination, and reap the rewards of your effort. Morita, a Japanese therapist, refers to effort as being good fortune.[29]

REWARDING PROGRESS

It is crucial that you build in celebrations and reward your progress. These rewards may be as simple as engaging in activities you enjoy, such as reading, watching movies or catching up with friends. In addition you may like to plan more elaborate celebrations when you reach important destinations in your journey. Gaining an audience to your successes is important and filling in people about the new you can be pivotal in stabilising your new identity as a person who has let go of their stress and anxiety.

Where to from here?

Well done for reaching the end of this chapter. Sometimes it is helpful for relatives to read this sort of information too, so that they can better understand what you are experiencing.

The next chapter is about taking action – one step at a time. It will talk about breaking down your journey into achievable stages, and will guide you in how to take the first steps in managing stress and anxiety. We will start teaching you some useful early strategies for managing stress and anxiety.

It is worth re-reading each chapter later on, as you often pick up different pieces of information as you re-read. Also, you may choose to continue to work through this guide on your own, or you may decide to seek some further assistance, whether that is by taking a course or finding a therapist.

TRAVEL REMINDERS

Here are some reminders from this chapter. You may want to copy them and make them into a reminder card to place in your diary or wallet, or even on the fridge or a mirror at home.

- You are not alone, and there is *hope*.
- Stress and anxiety are common.
- You are a unique individual – use your expert knowledge on your journey, and develop your 'travel kit' with the help of this guide.
- Stress leads to protective responses in the mind and body.
- Different factors (external and internal) can trigger stress.
- Anxiety is real and is not harmful.
- There are many strategies which can help.

TRAVEL DIARY

TAKE ACTION – ONE STEP AT A TIME

The journey of a thousand miles begins with one step.

—Lao Tzu (from *Tao Te Ching*, 4th–6th century BC)

This chapter will provide more information for the early part of your journey in managing stress and anxiety. You will find that each chapter in this guide builds on the previous one. For example, we might provide some information on a particular topic in one chapter; in the next we might provide some additional information on the same topic; and in the next we might talk about how this information relates to a helpful skill in managing stress and anxiety. In this way, we believe that the information presented and strategies described will be more understandable and useful to you.

In this chapter we will talk about breaking down your journey into achievable steps, and we will discuss how to take the first steps in managing stress and anxiety. We talk about baby steps, one small step at a time, as this is what we have found to be the best approach. We will outline some of the current models of therapy for stress and anxiety. We have endeavoured to select those which are based on evidence from research or fit with current thinking, and those which we have found most helpful in clinical practice.

Towards the end of this chapter we will introduce one useful technique, namely effective breathing. This technique can give you a sense of action and success early on. It will also lead into the next chapter, which covers lifestyle issues in stress and anxiety.

Where do I begin my journey?

Taking the first step on what may be a long journey can be very daunting. Asking you to actually do something about the stress and anxiety may seem as achievable as asking you to fly to the moon. Incredibly, 20 July 2009 was the 40th anniversary of the first humans flying to and landing on the moon. Remember Neil Armstrong's famous words: 'That's one small step for man, one giant leap for mankind.'[1] The moon landing reminds us that amazing things can be done when we put our minds to them. Imagine what it would have been like to contemplate the first journey to the moon. This was a journey never undertaken by humans before.

What qualities do you think the astronauts drew on within themselves to help them complete the journey successfully?

_____

_____

_____

_____

_____

_____

Travel involves change!

We have often had people consult with us wanting to change someone important in their lives, whether the 'someone' is a partner, child, parent or friend. These people are always disappointed to hear that you cannot change another person. However, the good news is you can change yourself. It is funny to note that usually people have more enthusiasm and energy for arguing why someone else should change their behaviour rather than why they should change themselves!

It makes much more sense to invest your time and effort in changing your own behaviour rather than someone else's, for a number of reasons. Firstly, you have the most say over yourself and your own behaviour. Secondly, if you change yourself, often the people closest to you have to change as well because you are no longer interacting with them in the same old patterns.

At this point, we would like you to consider several questions:

What makes you feel that it might be time for a change in your behaviour?

_____

_____

_____

_____

_____

_____

_____

By reading this book, you have taken the first step in changing. You may have taken other steps too. What qualities in you enabled you to take these steps?

_____

_____

_____

_____

_____

_____

Well done for taking these early steps. We understand that you have already made an effort in this journey. We also understand that sometimes individuals have mixed feelings about changing. That is understandable, because we become comfortable with how things are. However, we suspect that there is likely to be a sense of discomfort (either small or large) within you about the degree of stress or anxiety you are experiencing at the moment. That will help to motivate you along the way.[2]

We are also aware that at times other people can resist change in people close to them. It may be helpful to visualise a close group of people (or a family) as a set of cogs in a machine. Most of the time the cogs follow the same old pattern, each cog being driven by the cog alongside it. If that cog alongside decides to change and move in a different direction the other cogs may resist for a while, but in the end they will have to fit in with the cog that is maintaining consistent change. Similarly, some people may provide some resistance to the changes you are trying to make, because they are getting some kind of benefit from the old you, or perhaps they just don't like change. However, if you are persistent in the changes you are making eventually they will need to adapt to the new you in some way.

THE STEPS REQUIRED FOR CHANGE

We believe that people can change. We could not, in good conscience, do our jobs if we didn't believe people can change. There are, however, a number of steps that are needed for people to change:

Step 1: The person has a desire to change.

Step 2: The person believes that they can change.

Step 3: There is some assistance, which may be in the form of this book, or a therapist or a group programme.

Step 4: There is a plan for change, broken down into 'baby' steps.

Step 5: The person effectively monitors the change so that feedback can be given, and successes can be celebrated and reinforced.[3]

Making your travel plans

If you are planning a trip, you spend time thinking about where you want to go and why. You would also plan how you would get there and what you wanted to take. It is the same in planning for change in life, such as managing stress or anxiety. Part of this planning involves thinking about what change is necessary, and why it is important to you as an individual. It is also important to have a clear idea of the steps you are going to take in order to manage the stress and anxiety in your life.

This planning process takes time and you might need to have a few goes at it. You may want to read this section and take time to consider the questions, or even do it with someone else. A useful way of starting your travel plan is to consider what you value in life, or what is important to you.[4] This may relate to what you want your life to be about, what sort of person you want to be, or what relationships you want to build.

One of the therapies that we utilise is Acceptance and Commitment Therapy (ACT). This therapy encompasses different areas or domains in life, namely:

- family and friends
- romance or intimate relationships
- health and your body
- education and personal development
- work and finance
- leisure
- citizenship or community life
- environment or nature
- spirituality.[5]

You might like to consider your values in relation to each of these domains. We suggest that you use Table 5 opposite, which has these domain headings, and under each heading list what is important to you. For example, under the heading of work, having a job and job satisfaction might be important. Under leisure, you might value playing football with mates, or going to craft classes. Write these lists first.

The next step is to notice that in some of the domains you will probably feel your current life is pretty consistent with what you value. For example, you may value spending time with family and friends and that may be what is happening. However, in other areas, there may be a gap between what is important to you and what is currently happening; for example, you may value fitness but currently do not spend much time doing exercise. Make a note of these gaps in the table too.

TABLE 5: LIFE DOMAINS AND YOUR VALUES

Domain	What is important to you/what do you value in this domain?	Is there a gap between what is currently happening and what you value?
Family and friends		
Romance/intimate relationships		
Health and your body		
Education and personal development		
Work and finance		
Leisure (for example, hobbies, relaxation time)		
Citizenship/ community life (such as helping a neighbour, volunteering)		
Environment or nature		
Spirituality		

HAVING COMPLETED THIS TABLE, CONSIDER THE FOLLOWING QUESTIONS:

Which of these value areas or domains are particularly important to you at this time? Which domains do you need to focus on at the moment? Is it perhaps your health, finding time for leisure activities or exploring spirituality? Write down your ideas here.

_____

_____

_____

_____

_____

THESE IDEAS WILL HELP YOU FOCUS YOUR GOALS. THERE ARE ALSO SOME OTHER QUESTIONS WHICH MIGHT BE HELPFUL TO CONSIDER:

Firstly, how would your life be different if you let go of the stress and anxiety? (For example, what would you be able to do that is difficult now?)

_____

_____

_____

_____

_____

Also, are you neglecting any of the domains at the moment?

_____

_____

_____

_____

_____

_____

Now think about living a life with less stress and anxiety – would you be able to live a life more consistent with your values (for example, in the relationship or work domains)? We anticipate that your answer may well be 'yes'. We can all work on our life being more consistent with our values, and in doing so we can also find a greater sense of purpose and meaning.[6]

The first part of your journey towards letting go of stress and anxiety is setting your direction of travel. We ask you to keep the different domains and your own values in mind as these will guide your goals.[7] Now think about the sort of outcomes that you desire in relation to one domain to begin with. For example, if you have been neglecting your health and body, you might want to focus on this area. You would then think about what you value in this area, and if this is fitness, for example, you might choose to work on this through regular exercise. Or if, because of stress or anxiety, you have been neglecting friendships which are important to you, you might aim to gradually get back in touch with your friends. Working towards these outcomes will involve setting some personal aims or goals, and that is what we are going to look at next.

Your destination aims or goals

Have you thought about your direction of travel or destination in this journey? In the context of your journey in recovering from stress and anxiety, the destination relates to your aims or goals. Below are some useful guidelines for setting these. Remember to keep in mind the life domains that you have identified as being important to you and needing some work, and think about goals related to these areas.

- Make a list of the goals you wish to achieve.
- Prioritise these goals by choosing the one you have the most energy and enthusiasm for right now.
- Break down the prioritised goal into small steps.
- Write the time, day and date you will take the first small step.
- Write how you will know that you have achieved your goal.

There are also some guidelines for deciding on goals generally.

- Steps need to be specific, clear and small.
- Steps need to be expressed in positive terms. For example, 'I will go to the shopping centre once a week.' Not, 'I will stop avoiding the shopping centre.'
- Steps can be achieved alone and are not reliant on someone else. For example, 'I will go to the movies once a week, regardless of whether my friend comes with me.'
- Steps need to be realistic and achievable.[8]

To assist you in developing your aims or goals, here is an example of goal setting, beginning with Isabella's story.

ISABELLA'S STORY

Isabella feels nervous when she needs to speak in front of her fellow students at university, and she is especially anxious when she has to speak or present in front of her tutorial class. She worries that the other students will think she is 'stupid' and that they will wonder how she got into university.

Isabella doesn't talk in tutorials. She often feels ill on tutorial days and has missed the last two. Initially, Isabella feels a great relief when she decides to avoid the tutorial and then she spends the rest of the day feeling sad and disappointed about not going. For the rest of the day she worries about what work she has missed and whether she is going to fail the subject because of missing too much work.

Basically, Isabella is robbing herself of the chance to be successful. If she keeps on avoiding the opportunity to speak to her tutorial class she will never realise that she can do it and it is not as bad as she believes it is. In addition, the more Isabella avoids the situation, the more she believes she cannot cope. Isabella's avoidance behaviours are unfortunately heading towards confirming her worst fear, that she cannot cope with university-level work. Using the planning sheet below, Isabella can start to address what she wants, which is to attend tutorials, contribute to discussion and ultimately give a talk in the tutorial.

Isabella wants to change her behaviours and feel less anxious about tutorials. She could use a planning sheet such as the one overleaf to guide her in changing the behaviours.

PLANNING SHEET: MY PLAN FOR CHANGE

My aim is: _____

My first step is: _____

My second step is: _____

My third step is: _____

My fourth step is: _____

How will I benefit from achieving this goal?_____

The time, day, date I will take that first step is: _____

I plan to achieve my goal by: _____

I will know I have achieved it because: _____

My reward to myself will be: _____

When Isabella completes the planning sheet, it might look like the one below. Isabella could follow the plan to assist her in her efforts to change and to feel more confident.

ISABELLA'S PLAN FOR CHANGE

My aim is: to contribute to discussion in my tutorial class.

My first step is: to read about the tutorial topic.

My second step is: to practise saying things about the topic in front of the mirror at home.

My third step is: to use calming breathing exercises before the class.

My fourth step is: to approach a fellow student who looks friendly and discuss the tutorial topic before the class to gain confidence.

My fifth step is: to make a small verbal contribution to the tutorial.

How will I benefit from achieving this goal? I won't feel sick and worried as much and won't miss my tutorials.

The time, day, date I will take that first step is: now.

I plan to achieve my goal by: next week.

I will know I have achieved it because: I will have contributed to a tutorial.

My reward to myself will be: to tell my best friends and go out with them.

Blocks in the road

Goal setting seems easy and sensible when you read it in a book like this. However, if change were that easy you probably would have done it by yourself already! The reason it can be more difficult is that you may come across some road blocks that can stop you from reaching your destination or goal, and it is worth contemplating alternative routes and back-up plans to deal with these.

STRESS AND ANXIETY

It seems ludicrous but the biggest road block to you travelling away from stress and anxiety will probably be not wanting to feel stressed or anxious! We often talk to clients about short-term pain for long-term gain versus short-term gain for long-term pain. What we mean is that it may be necessary to feel some uncomfortable feelings of stress and anxiety in the short-term in order for a longer-term better outcome of having a more fulfilling life that is not driven by stress and anxiety. Alternatively, we can escape the uncomfortable feelings of stress and anxiety in the short term by employing avoidance strategies (such as not putting ourselves in certain situations, or using alcohol or drugs), but the long-term consequences of this short-term gain may be a lifestyle you do not enjoy or feel good about.

GOAL SETTING

Many people find even the words 'goal setting' quite intimidating. We toyed with the idea of replacing these words with less threatening ones, but in the end decided it is probably better to keep the useful aspects of these words at the forefront of the reader's mind and challenge some of the more negative aspects of them. Goal setting is a way of travelling towards the things we want for our life. Goals need to be clear. They can help give us control, meaning, purpose and a sense of direction. They also provide a clear structure for change when things may feel confusing. Working towards important goals can help increase feelings of mastery, focus and motivation, and decrease feelings of helplessness.[9]

EASY

People often come to therapy hoping for the quick fix, magic pill or magic wand. When someone asks us how to manage stress or anxiety, they may really be asking whether there's an easy way to deal with these issues. Chances are they have already worked out many ways to manage stress and anxiety, but have found them hard work. This book will probably make the way a bit easier, but ultimately most achievements of importance in life require a certain amount of effort.

FEAR

In *The Note Book of Elbert Hubbard*, Elbert Hubbard wrote that 'the greatest mistake you can make in life is to be continually fearing you will make one'.[10] Fear can be a powerful force that keeps us stuck. Common fears include:

fear of failure, fear of change, fear of feeling stressed and anxious, fear of being embarrassed and fear of making a mistake or being wrong. However, it is important to be prepared to try different strategies, knowing that some of these strategies won't work. By learning what doesn't work we become clearer about what will work.

INSTANT GRATIFICATION

One of the main ways we learn is through cause and effect. We behave in a certain way and it has consequences. If we deem the consequences to be positive then that behaviour is reinforced and we tend to repeat it to get the same effect. If the consequence is negative we may try to stop engaging in that behaviour. However, this relationship becomes difficult when the consequence of our behaviour is not experienced soon after the action. A good example is trying to lose weight. You may eat healthy food and exercise for weeks before you actually see a positive result such as a decrease in kilos on the scale. This can be disheartening and can lead you to believe that your strategies for weight loss are not working. But if you stick with them, they may well lead to good results.

Strategies for managing stress and anxiety can be similar to the weight loss scenario. They may take a while to produce results but with perseverance, practice and the correct technique, they will work. Similarly, successful weight loss and maintenance of that weight loss is all about changing to a healthy lifestyle in the long term, not just a quick fix. The same is true of stress management: it is long-term lifestyle change that will provide the best results.

Many people give up good, useful strategies prematurely because they are not getting instant results. An expectation of 'instant gratification' or immediate positive results may make it hard for us to set goals and then follow through on them, especially if we have to experience some uncomfortable feelings before we experience the benefits. Try not to be pushed around by a sense of urgency to change instantly. Our experience is that the more gradual the change, the more likely it is that the change will be maintained over time.

FRUSTRATION

We tend to feel comfortable with what we know or what is familiar, even if it is essentially uncomfortable. For example, we may work in a particular place for many years, despite a critical boss or dreams of doing something different. As a result of this tendency to stick with the familiar, we may find it difficult to initiate and maintain change, and we may feel frustrated. Interestingly, an unknown author wrote that the definition of frustration is 'trying the same thing over and over again and expecting a different outcome'. Can you relate to this in any way?

LOW SELF-ESTEEM

Self-esteem describes your sense of self-worth. It refers to how you see and judge yourself, often in comparison to others. Low self-esteem can affect how you function in daily life and how you relate to other people.[11] It can interfere with the journey you are taking with this book, as this journey involves trying different strategies which may be challenging at times or involve how we relate to others. This is why we will discuss the idea of self-esteem in greater detail later in the book, and challenge some of the taken-for-granted beliefs about self-esteem. We will also introduce the concept of self-acceptance and self-compassion as an alternative to self-esteem in Chpater 8. Just remember, you have started this journey and that took effort and courage. Persist and you will see improvement in many areas, including your self-esteem.

LACK OF TIME OR RESOURCES

Sometimes lack of time or resources can interfere with your journey. Always refer back to your aims and goals to remind yourself why this journey is important. The beauty of this journey is it can be taken one step at a time, and we suggest that you allocate small amounts of time regularly to it. If you need to go back and re-read and repeat a step in the journey, that is okay, and may actually be beneficial. Remember that you are important, and this is an important journey for you. Effort and persistence are your two greatest resources.

UNSUPPORTIVE FAMILY AND FRIENDS

As we said earlier in this chapter, some people may provide resistance to the changes you are trying to make. They may even sabotage your efforts to change. However, if you are persistent in the changes you are making, eventually they will need to adapt to the 'new you' in some way.

Means of travel — approaches to stress and anxiety

In the first chapter, we spoke of taking a holistic approach when dealing with anxiety and stress. This involves addressing your lifestyle issues, such as healthy eating and exercise, sleep and relaxation, interests and laughter. It involves taking time to nurture your body, mind and spirit. The term 'holistic' also relates to the choice of therapeutic approaches to stress and anxiety. We utilise a number of different models of therapy, as they each have valuable approaches to stress and anxiety and useful skills to learn. We have found that each individual is different and will relate to different approaches. It may be useful for you to have an understanding of the different approaches so that if you decide to work with a therapist, you can ask them about which approaches they use.

The psychological therapies which we have drawn upon in writing this guide are:

- Multimodal Therapy
- Motivational Interviewing
- Cognitive Behavioural Therapy
- Narrative Therapy
- Relaxation Therapy
- Hypnotherapy
- Mindfulness
- Constructive Living
- Acceptance and Commitment Therapy.

In this section we will briefly outline each of these therapeutic approaches. In later chapters we will discuss what we find valuable in relation to these approaches and letting go of stress and anxiety. You may recognise also that we have already tapped into several of these approaches in the first two chapters of this guide.

MULTIMODAL THERAPY
The overall approach taken in this guide is based on a model of psychological therapy called Multimodal Therapy. This was developed by Arnold Lazarus, who recognised that individuals are unique and have different biological make-ups and personalities.[12] In Multimodal Therapy, health professionals or therapists choose strategies or skills from several different therapy models when working with the individual with stress or anxiety, depending on the issues of that individual. In other words, the therapist asks, 'What is best for this particular person?'[13]

MOTIVATIONAL INTERVIEWING

Motivational Interviewing (MI) is a directive, client-centred counselling style that has been shown to be effective in its aim to bring about behaviour change.[14] Sometimes we feel ambivalent about change or resist change. We might have a degree of comfort in how things are, but there might be discomfort about changing too. MI helps individuals to explore and resolve this ambivalence. In MI the therapist avoids acting as an 'expert'. They listen and understand, but recognise that the individual needs to determine their own direction and goals.[15]

The therapist aims to pick up any discrepancy between what the individual values or aims to change and the current problem behaviour. For example, an individual might use smoking as a way of dealing with stress. However, they might be worried about the effect of smoking on their lungs. The therapist would help them identify these views, perhaps by looking at a future with the behaviour still present and one with the behaviour absent. They would also help the individual feel more confident that they can change, help them plan change and feel more optimistic about the change.[16,17] We incorporated MI principles in our section on goal setting.

COGNITIVE BEHAVIOURAL THERAPY

Many of you would have heard or read about Cognitive Behavioural Therapy (CBT), which is often used to help individuals manage stress or anxiety. There have been quite a few books written about CBT, and there is strong research evidence that CBT is an effective therapy in dealing with anxiety.[18]

So what is CBT? It refers to a set of ideas and strategies which are based on the view that thoughts (or cognitions) and beliefs affect our feelings and behaviour, and are in turn affected by them.[19] In fact, we all have fairly constant streams of thoughts, and many of these thoughts happen automatically; that is, they just seem to pop into our mind. For example, an individual might be given a number of new tasks at work and have thoughts such as, 'This is too much . . . I'm sure I will make a mess of it . . . what if I lose my job?' This individual is likely to feel worried and down, might not be able to go to sleep, and may become snappy with others at work. You can see in this example that the individual's thoughts, feelings and behaviour are interrelated.

Learning how thinking and feeling interact, and how to develop different ways of thinking, is the basis of the cognitive part of CBT. In CBT, the therapist works together with the client to guide them through strategies related to the thought processes, such as identifying which thoughts are helpful and which are unhelpful, and then learning to challenge and correct the unhelpful ones.[20] Underlying beliefs are also examined. For example, in anxiety, negative beliefs might relate to a sense of being threatened and lacking the ability to deal with threats.[21] Strategies are then provided to assist the individual to develop more helpful beliefs.[22]

CBT also utilises a number of techniques associated with behaviours, such as engaging in activities, relaxation and assertiveness training.[23, 24] This is the behavioural arm of CBT, and many practise behavioural therapy in its own right. This is particularly helpful in anxiety disorders and problems such as gambling. CBT informs our daily practice, and we have outlined the CBT model in Chapter 4.

NARRATIVE THERAPY

Narrative Therapy involves the therapist and the individual working together to identify what the individual wants in their own life, and how best to utilise their own knowledge and skills to achieve that. The therapist views the conversations with the individual as central to the therapeutic process, attending carefully to the language used. The therapist is curious about the individual's context and their stories. Together the therapist and the individual can co-create a new story. [25]

A number of techniques are used in narrative therapy, such as 'externalising' the problem. For example, the stress or anxiety is highlighted as the problem, rather than the individual being the problem. You will notice that throughout this book, we refer to 'the anxiety', which reflects the narrative approach of externalising the issue – that is, you are not the problem, 'the anxiety' is the problem. We describe narrative approaches and techniques in detail in Chapter 7.

RELAXATION THERAPY
Relaxation is the opposite response of the body and mind to the stress response. Relaxation Therapy utilises techniques aimed at relaxing both physically and mentally, and these techniques can help reduce stress and anxiety. We can all learn to relax more effectively. Relaxation techniques require practice, but we only need to invest ten to twenty minutes regularly to see the benefits. There is a range of techniques which will be outlined later in this book. It is worth trying them all as you may find one technique suits you better than another. Meditation is a state of relaxation created by focusing attention and quietening the mind. We explore Relaxation Therapy further in Chapter 3.

HYPNOTHERAPY
Hypnosis is another useful therapeutic tool. Hypnosis refers to an altered state of consciousness or a trance state, different from sleep and different from being awake. It is similar to

relaxation or meditation. The brain wave pattern changes in hypnosis, fluctuating between alpha and delta waves. The mind regularly goes into a brief hypnotic state to relax and refresh brain function.

In hypnosis, the mind is more open to suggestion, and this is the basis of its use as a therapy. The hypnotherapist can assist the individual in managing thoughts, emotions or behaviours through suggestion. Hypnosis is commonly used for relaxation and stress management or to change behaviours (such as smoking). A number of other therapeutic approaches can be combined with hypnosis, such as CBT. Also, the individual will usually be taught self-hypnosis as part of the therapy.

MINDFULNESS

Mindfulness refers to paying purposeful attention to the present moment. It stems from Buddhist and Hindu practices. In his professional life, John Kabat-Zinn has focused on developing and researching a number of treatment programmes on mindfulness.[26] For example, in the 1980s, Acceptance and Commitment Therapy (ACT) was developed, incorporating mindfulness and behaviour change strategies.

A variety of mindfulness techniques can assist the individual to relax and let go of stress and anxiety. These include mindful breathing, specific mindfulness meditations or everyday mindfulness (such as being in the present moment when doing simple activities such as having a cup of tea or walking). We have drawn on mindfulness techniques in several chapters in this book (including chapters 3, 4 and 6).

Mindfulness has come under much greater attention in recent years, in relation to 'neuroplasticity' of the brain, an exciting concept that was introduced in Chapter 1. When we practise mindfulness, we are activating neurons in our brain and stimulating growth.[27] This is why several newer psychological approaches, such as Mindfulness-based CBT (MBCT) and ACT, incorporate mindfulness.

CONSTRUCTIVE LIVING

The Constructive Living approach suggests that constantly focusing on feelings and aiming for a constantly happy, anxiety-free life will actually cause additional suffering. It proposes that we accept or acknowledge whatever feelings, good or bad, that come our way and then get on with life. Constructive Living suggests that, as it is hard to control our feelings directly, we should not use them as the foundation on which to build our life.[28]

Constructive Living is about recognising what you feel but doing what is considered to be best anyway. It recommends dealing with feelings by waiting – over time they will disappear in some moments and emerge in others in different intensity. Feelings should not be ignored as they can give us information about what needs to be done. However, we don't need to constantly pay attention to them. There are three themes in Constructive Living, namely to accept reality, know your purpose and do what needs to be done or take action.[29]

ACCEPTANCE AND COMMITMENT THERAPY

As mentioned, ACT is a form of behaviour therapy which encourages connection with the present moment (mindfulness) and clarifying and connecting with our values. It aims to help the individual handle painful thoughts and feelings, and to create a rich and meaningful life through action. Rather than evaluating thoughts, it encourages us to view thoughts as a series of words or stories.[30] ACT encourages the acceptance of distressing emotions or events, or in other words, a willingness to experience them, without trying to change or control them.

It utilises techniques such as cognitive defusion (including observing thoughts or thanking the mind for a thought, or singing the thought) to assist acceptance.[31] These will be explained in more detail in Chapter 6.

Medications

Medications may be part of treatment for anxiety. Your GP can discuss the different types of medication with you. The most common anti-anxiety medications used now are the selective serotonin re-uptake inhibitors (SSRIs). These are antidepressants but are also very effective in anxiety. They include fluoxetine (trade name: Prozac), sertraline (Lustral), citalopram (Cipramil) or escitalopram (Cipralex). Other antidepressants which might be used for anxiety are venlafaxine (Efexor) and duloxetine (Cymbalta). Choice of medication will depend on the individual person and the characteristics of the anxiety, and whether there is co-existent depression.

These drugs may take several weeks to work. If prescribed, it is important to take the tablets regularly and for long enough to give them a good chance of working for you. Like other medications, these drugs can potentially have side effects. SSRIs, for example, may cause sleepiness, nausea or headaches. It is best to start at a low dose and build up slowly with these medications, as this helps avoid unwanted side effects. Side effects often lessen over the first few weeks, and so it is worth persevering. Talk with your doctor if you have any queries about side effects. Dosage will depend on the individual and their response to treatment.[32]

Other guidelines include not stopping taking the antidepressants without talking with your GP (as the dose needs to be tapered down). Also, if you need to use another type of medication and you are taking these medications it is important to check with your GP or pharmacist first. These drugs may also interact with some complementary medicines such as St John's Wort, which can cause troublesome symptoms and should be avoided. Take care with drinking alcohol while taking antidepressants; it is generally advised that you reduce the amount of alcohol, or abstain.[33]

Complementary therapies

Some individuals prefer to try natural remedies ahead of synthetic drugs. Complementary therapies for anxiety include St John's Wort, passionflower and valerian. There is some evidence regarding the effectiveness of each of these natural substances, but studies are often limited by study size or methodology.[34] However, they are certainly worth considering and discussing with your GP or naturopath.

Practices such as yoga, tai chi, massage, aromatherapy, creative activities and music are often considered as complementary therapies in managing stress and anxiety.[35] For example, massage is one of the oldest forms of healing, used since ancient times. It is increasingly utilised by people today. We suggest that you explore these activities if they appeal to you, are meaningful to you or if you find them helpful.

Breathing to relax along the way

Now that you have an understanding of some of the broad models of therapy, we will begin to share some specific skills that can be useful early in your travels. A good skill to begin with is breathing. When you think about it, breathing is probably the most central thing to life as we need to breathe to survive. When experiencing stress and anxiety, our breathing rates can alter. People commonly report a sense of breathlessness, especially when experiencing panic. Breathing skills can help you feel more calm and relaxed, and can stop more physical anxiety symptoms from developing.

Breathing techniques are important in learning to relax, because, for example, in times of stress an individual's breathing rate may increase and breathing can become shallow. This is called hyperventilation. The usual resting breathing rate in an adult is about 12 breaths per minute, but when anxious this may go up to 25 breaths per minute. Shallow breathing reduces the level of carbon dioxide in the circulation. This can make the blood more alkaline and restrict the blood vessels, causing dizziness and headache.[36] Breathing techniques can be used to slow the breathing rate and lessen shallow breathing.[37]

The larger volumes of the lungs are at the base of the lungs, and so effective breathing means expanding your chest by lowering your diaphragm – in doing so the abdomen moves outwards. Often we think taking a full breath involves raising the shoulders, but this is not the case as this is where the smaller volumes of the lungs are. We suggest that you take medium-sized breaths and focus on expanding the chest (rather than lifting the shoulders). At the same time you will feel the abdomen move. Sometimes it helps to imagine the abdomen is like a balloon, and when you breathe in you fill the balloon. This is known as abdominal or diaphragmatic breathing, and you will find abdominal breathing is used in activities such as yoga and tai chi, and in many meditation techniques.

When we travel we often take several items which we need and rely on. Those items might be a passport or some soap. What follows are several breathing techniques for you to try. In our experience most people find these very helpful and enjoyable, and so they become some of the key 'items' you will need as you recover.

BREATHING EXERCISES

Set aside some time to try the following breathing exercises. As with everything we learn, practice is essential. Don't expect to do them perfectly the first time. Set aside a few minutes every day to practise, or preferably several times a day. You might like to keep a record of your practice for a week or two, as this can help keep you on track. An example of the sort of record we suggest is provided in the next chapter.

ABDOMINAL BREATHING EXERCISE

Try abdominal, or diaphragmatic, breathing while sitting, standing or lying (depending on what suits you). Whichever position you choose, ensure your back is straight yet relaxed. Place your hands over your abdomen, and let them relax. As you breathe in feel the hands move out, then breathe out and feel them move in. Take gentle, medium breaths, rather than really deep breaths. Then repeat this process and try breathing 'in, two, three; out, two, three'.

Make an effort to pause and focus on your breath in ways such as this several times during the day.

AWARE BREATHING EXERCISE

Breathe in and out through your nose if comfortable with this, or in through the nose and out through the mouth. Simply be aware of the breath in and then the breath out. Breathe at a gentle, slow pace, and feel the cooler air moving in. Breathe out and feel the warmer air move out. Repeat several times. You might like to incorporate saying 'relax', 'peace' or 'calm' in your mind as you breathe out, and focus on letting go of tension and stress each time you breathe out.[38]

MINDFUL BREATHING EXERCISE

Observe and feel the breath. Rest your attention where the air enters and leaves the body, whether that be through the nose or the mouth. Maintain your focus on this for a few minutes. During this exercise, distracting thoughts or images may come into your mind. There is no need to try to stop these thoughts coming into the mind. Simply notice them, and let them pass, allowing the attention to return gently to an awareness of the breath.[39]

COUNTING THE BREATH EXERCISE

Count one on your first in-breath and one on your first out-breath, then two on the next in-breath and two on the next out-breath, and so on. Or you may want to note the breath, the 'in' and the 'out' of the breath. Think 'in' as you breathe in, and 'out' as you breathe out. Keep doing this until you reach ten then start again at one. [40]

These breathing techniques will help you focus simply on the breath, and let go of thoughts or concerns. As a result, they will help you feel calmer in yourself. Again, practice is vital. These breathing techniques become easier as you practise and become more familiar with them. Start with just a few minutes, and gradually increase your time relaxing.

TRAVEL REMINDERS

Here are some reminders from this chapter. You may want to copy them and make them into a reminder card to place in your diary or wallet, or even on the fridge or a mirror at home.

- It is important to break down your journey into small, manageable, steps.
- It can be useful to think about what change is necessary for you, and why it is important to you as an individual.
- What are your goals or aims on this journey? Remember, they need to be specific, clear, expressed in positive terms, not reliant on someone else, realistic and achievable.
- Certain things can get in the way of your travel away from stress and anxiety, including the effort needed to manage stress and anxiety, various fears, feeling disheartened or frustrated, lack of time and resources or support. Remember, change often takes time!
- There are many strategies which can help. Breathing techniques are one of the first strategies to learn and use on this journey.

TRAVEL DIARY

HOW TO REDUCE YOUR STRESS BUCKET

Every now and then go away, have a little relaxation. For when you come back to your work, your judgement will be surer; since to remain constantly at work will cause you to lose the power of judgement. Go some distance away, because the work appears small and more of it can be taken in at a glance; and a lack of harmony or proportion is more readily seen.

—Leonardo da Vinci (1452–1519)

In Chapter 1 we defined stress as a response to a demand which we are experiencing, such as dealing with a difficult teenager, meeting work deadlines or giving a speech. In addition, stress is an individual experience, and has different meanings to different people because they perceive different demands in different ways.

Stress occurs when the body responds to changes in the outside or inside environment that are perceived as a demand. Stress consists of:

- the stressor – the demand or change (for example, a snarling dog)
- how the stressor is perceived (scary or non-scary)
- the stress response in the body and mind (fight or flight response).[1]

The fight or flight response

The fight or flight response occurs in any situation that is perceived as a threat. Remember the primitive man in Chapter 1 who was saved from the sabre-toothed tiger by his body's ability to prepare him to flee or fight the tiger? Once our caveman had run away from the tiger and dealt with this threat, his body would have returned to a relaxed or unstressed state as the build-up of energy was discharged. Therefore, if we visualise a spectrum where the fight or flight response is at one end, the relaxation response would be at the opposite end of that spectrum.

Unfortunately, our stressors these days are not as straightforward as a tiger. In today's world we cannot always fight or run away from stressful situations, such as financial worries, marital strain or work issues. Consequently, the energy that is built up in the fight or flight response to these stressors does not get used, and the body never fully returns to its relaxed or unstressed state. This can sometimes lead a person to become totally disconnected from feelings of relaxation in their body and mind.

If we think about that caveman from Chapter 1 and we believe in natural selection over human generations, it makes sense that the humans with the best fight or flight response would have survived and had children. As the generations went on it follows that this fight or flight response would have been handed down genetically and become more highly tuned and responsive. So perhaps today's generation of humans has a fight or flight response that has the potential to be 'too good'. Over many years our fight or flight response can become over-sensitive so that it starts perceiving too many things as threats. It becomes a bit like a car alarm system that has been set too sensitively. The car alarm system should be sounding its alert when someone is tampering with the car door, but instead it is being triggered by a person walking metres away in the opposite direction who is posing no real threat to the car's security at all.

In people, this over-sensitivity can express itself as their fight or flight response being triggered by worries that do not pose a real threat to their safety. For example, worries about what other people think of them, concerns about how they look or even anxieties about things that have not happened yet. Perceiving lots of things as threats and not being able to relax your body and mind can lead some people to feel such a build-up of stress that it does not take very much for them to feel completely overwhelmed. We have found it useful to use the idea of the 'stress bucket' to help people understand what may be happening in their body and mind when their stress levels are rising.

The stress bucket

Have you ever seen someone express strong emotions by screaming, shouting, or crying? What sorts of thoughts go through your head? Are there thoughts like, 'What's going on? Something really bad must have happened!' Maybe you're also feeling a little anxious as you watch to see how the situation unfolds, and perhaps you're wondering whether you can help. What happens when you find out that the person is reacting this way because she has broken a fingernail? All of a sudden you go through an immediate reassessment of your first impressions of the situation. Perhaps phrases such as 'meltdown', 'lost it', 'out of control' or 'how embarrassing' go through your mind. Maybe you are thinking, 'I'm glad it's not me.' But with some further thought you realise that the broken fingernail is probably not what the person is reacting to, but that it happens to be the proverbial 'straw that broke the camel's back' – or what we like to call 'the last drop in the stress bucket'.

The stress bucket is a metaphor we like to use to illustrate how stress can build up and before you know it you are 'spilling over' with emotions and behaviours that do not fit with the person you want to be. We have defined stress as demands made upon us. Every day of our lives we have many demands made upon us. For example, we have to get up in the morning, get washed, have breakfast, and possibly feed children and get them ready for the day. If you imagine yourself as a bucket with a finite capacity for stress and you imagine that every demand made upon you is a drop of stress in your bucket, then you can probably imagine how easy it would be for that bucket to overflow. Let's take the example of Lily.

LILY'S STORY

Lily has been struggling to gain a sense of work-life balance. She believes that she must always be available to her boss in order to keep her job. Lily's mother has breast cancer and Lily organises her time away from work around her mother's medical appointments, shopping needs and cleaning requirements. Lily was given an expensive manicure voucher for her birthday six months ago but has not had time to go for the appointment. When she realised the voucher was about to expire she booked the appointment in between two different appointments for her mother, on her only day off in several months.

In the middle of the appointment she received an urgent phone call from her boss asking her to return to work as soon as possible. Lily tried to explain to her boss that she had other commitments but felt her boss would not take no for an answer, so she returned to work, leaving her mother waiting for her in the car. As Lily got out of the car, in the pouring rain, she stepped into a muddy puddle that reached the ankle of her favourite suede boots. When she got to the office, she discovered the emergency could have easily been dealt with by her boss, and as she took the necessary files out of the filing cabinet she broke her newly manicured nail and began to sob.

What do you think was the last drop in Lily's bucket? In what way did Lily react when her bucket started spilling over with stress?

_____

_____

_____

_____

_____

What do you think were the drops that had been filling up her bucket for a while?

_____

_____

_____

_____

_____

Have you ever overreacted to a situation and wondered what was going on? What signs and signals tell you that your stress bucket is getting dangerously full?

_____

_____

_____

_____

_____

How do I empty my stress bucket?

Life is full of demands, so everyone is going to have some stress in their bucket. Some people will have more than others because of their lifestyle, life circumstances, personality and how they view the world. However, there is something we can all do to lower the level of stress in our buckets so that we are not on the verge of spilling over the edge every time a new demand presents itself to us. This thing is called 'relaxation'. As we said before, relaxation is the opposite of the stress/fight or flight response and should happen automatically after we have dealt with a stressor. However, due to the ongoing nature of the types of stressors of modern life we have become disconnected with our natural relaxation response and need to relearn it.

WHAT IS RELAXATION?

The relaxation response is the body's own way of preventing overstress and stress-related problems. It could be said that we have lost this natural response due to the demands we make on ourselves and others, demands that have become part of modern life. The good news is that the relaxation response can be rediscovered or relearned with a little effort.

Relaxation is a way of producing a calm body and a quiet mind. People can lower the level of stress in their bucket by regular relaxation practice, so that when drops of stress are falling into your bucket (which they will, because life is stressful) you don't have to worry so much about 'spilling over'. In this way, relaxation is a good *preventative* strategy. We will talk more about this shortly.

Table 6 shows the relationship between the stress response and the relaxation response, and indicates the positive effects that relaxation can have on the body.

TABLE 6: RELATIONSHIP BETWEEN THE STRESS AND RELAXATION RESPONSES

Signs and symptoms of stress	Stress response	Relaxation response
Heart rate	Increased	Decreased
Blood pressure	Increased	Decreased
Breathing rate	Increased	Decreased
Muscle tension	Increased	Decreased
Sweating	Increased	Decreased
State of mental arousal	Increased	Decreased
Adrenaline flow	Increased	Decreased

WHAT DO I NEED TO DO TO RELAX?

We often look at relaxation training as a preventative measure rather than a cure. What we mean by this is that relaxation practice will work when you are stressed out (that is, when your stress bucket is about to overflow), but it is better to practise relaxation on a more regular basis so you are getting your stress levels to be much lower in your bucket. When beginning your relaxation practice, it is important to prepare yourself for relaxation as you want to maximise your chances of being able to successfully relax.

When we teach relaxation to someone for the first time we usually do it with them sitting in a chair because this position is easy to adapt to everyday life. For example, you can relax this way while sitting on a bus, while sitting at your desk at work or while sitting in a shopping centre. You might get a few inquiring glances if you started lying in the aisle in the bus! It is also less likely that you will fall asleep during relaxation training if sitting.

PREPARATION FOR RELAXATION
Here are some tips to follow when preparing for relaxation:

- Choose a special room in your house that you associate with good feelings to practise your relaxation.
- Do not eat a big meal before relaxation practice.
- Do not do relaxation directly after strenuous exercise.
- Go to the toilet before starting your relaxation.
- Try to ensure you will not be interrupted by taking the phone off the hook, informing others that you won't be available for a while, or putting a 'do not disturb' sign on the door.
- Make sure the room is not too hot or too cold.
- Turn down the lights, or turn them off.
- Remove contact lenses or glasses.
- Wear comfortable, loose clothing.

The relaxation position in a chair requires you to have your feet flat on the floor and your hands resting palms down on your thighs. We don't cross ankles or legs or clasp hands together because these small actions require some muscle tension, and these positions might disturb the blood supply. You might end up with hands or feet that feel numb or asleep!

If for some reason you cannot sit, it is okay to lie comfortably on the floor, bed or couch on your back with arms by your side, legs flat, and your neck supported.

CAUTIONS

There are some cautions with relaxation. Individuals who dissociate readily (for example, feel disjointed or out of the situation or their body), or those with active psychotic symptoms, should be very careful using these techniques. Also, those with severe depression may find concentrating on these techniques difficult. We suggest that you talk with your therapist as they know you and can guide you as to whether or not these techniques are appropriate for you.

How do I learn to relax?

There are many different relaxation techniques and most of them are based on two main things, namely slowing down your breathing and the loosening or relaxing of muscles. Relaxation techniques can be physical or mental or a combination of both. Also, different people will be able to relax in different ways. Some individuals relax through visual means, such as reading, movies, enjoying looking at trees or the ocean. Some relax through the 'auditory' sense or sound, such as nature sounds or music; and others like to relax through the 'kinesthetic' sense or movement – dance, walking, swimming or tai chi.

There are some basic techniques that everyone can learn and enjoy, and others can be matched to the individual. We will describe the basic ones first.

TIMING YOUR BREATH
As mentioned in Chapter 2, one of the easiest relaxation techniques involves slowing down your breathing rate. Try the

following exercise so you can get a baseline of your breathing rate.

TIMING YOUR BREATH EXERCISE

Time how many breaths you take in 1 minute and write the number on the line below. You might like to count your breath for 30 seconds and double the count. Also, note that the breath in and out is counted as one.

Breaths per minute:

_____

_____

_____

_____

The average breathing rate for an adult at rest tends to be 12 breaths per minute. For a person who is anxious the breathing rate can go up to 25 breaths per minute. You probably found that your breathing rate was a bit higher than 12 breaths. This is normal, as when we ask people to notice their breathing for the first time it tends to increase. It is nothing to be concerned about, and we asked you to do this exercise so you can gain a baseline of your breathing, as a way of measuring your relaxation training progress. You will find if you practise your breathing exercises regularly your breathing rate will stay at a lower level and this in turn will help keep the level of stress in your stress bucket lower. This form of relaxation is quick, easy and can be done in many different circumstances without any attention being drawn to what you are doing.

A BREATHING TECHNIQUE TO SLOW YOUR BREATH

A simple breathing technique that helps you slow down your breathing rate involves closing your mouth and taking a breath in through your nose for a count of three and then exhaling the breath through your nose for a count of three. Repeating this breathing pattern should result in 6-second breathing cycles. Breathing through the nose helps most people slow down their breathing naturally, but if you find it uncomfortable it is okay to breathe through your mouth. It is helpful to use a word to say to yourself in your mind as you exhale, such as 'relax', 'calm', 'peace' or whatever you find calming. In this way the word becomes strongly associated with your relaxed state and, with practice, simply saying that word can bring about the state of relaxation in your body and mind that we are working towards.

It is also helpful if you use diaphragmatic or abdominal breathing during this technique. The following technique will help you determine if you are using abdominal breathing.

ABDOMINAL BREATHING EXERCISE

Place the middle fingers of both hands on your stomach so they are lightly touching each other. As you breathe in your middle fingers should gently pull away from each other as your abdomen rises, and as you breathe out they will move to touch each other again as your abdomen falls. Another way to check you are breathing diaphragmatically is to lie down, put one hand on your abdomen and see if it is rising as you breathe in, just like an expanding balloon, and then see it fall as you exhale.

After this exercise, we suggest that you count your

breathing rate again. Write down the number of breaths per minute.

_____

Notice that this rate is probably lower than when you counted your breathing rate a few minutes ago.

PROGRESSIVE MUSCLE RELAXATION
Progressive muscle relaxation (PMR) is a good simple relaxation technique for beginners that combines the slowing of the breath and the letting go of tension in the muscles. The next exercise illustrates the difference between tensed and relaxed muscles.

TENSE MUSCLES EXERCISE
Make a fist with your right hand and hold it as tight as you can for 5 seconds. Then let go of the fist and shake out your fingers loosely.

Write down on the lines below what you noticed.

_____

_____

_____

Did you notice the tension in your fist, fingers and forearm? What was it like to then release the tension?

_____

_____

_____

Hopefully you found the relaxation sensation to be a pleasant one. The progressive muscle relaxation technique aims to help you relax in three different ways. First it helps you to develop slow, regular breathing as an aid to relaxation, as described above. Secondly it helps you to recognise the feelings of relaxation in each of your muscle groups and finally it helps you to associate the word 'relax' with feelings of physical relaxation. Therefore, eventually you can use the word 'relax' as a trigger for relaxing your body and mind.

Set aside some time to try the following PMR exercise. As with everything we learn, practice is essential. Don't expect to do it perfectly the first time. Set aside a few minutes every day to practise, or preferably several times a day.

PMR EXERCISE

Start by slowing down your breathing rate using the breathing technique described above and saying 'relax' to yourself as you exhale. To begin the technique you should be in the sitting relaxation position and let your eyes gently close. Then you might like to notice some of the sensations and feelings in your body right now. Systematically go through your muscle groups using the following prompts and let go of any feelings of tightness, and focus on increasing sensations of comfort and looseness in your muscles.

Notice the sensations in your toes and feet and let the relaxation flow like a gentle wave or stream up through your ankles, through the calf muscles, up through your thighs, right up to the tops of your legs. Maybe you can notice a gentle heaviness in your legs as they sink down into the chair comfortably.

Next, allow the gentle wave of relaxation to continue up

into the middle part of your body. Up through the buttock muscles, pelvis and stomach. Through the hips and into your lower back. Flowing at its own pace up through the back, up and down the spine.

The wave of relaxation continues gently flowing up into the chest, between your shoulder blades and into the shoulders.

Now let the relaxation flow into your neck and throat, progressing into your scalp and across your forehead. Now it flows down your face, around your eyes, into the cheeks, your mouth and jaw. Your teeth should be slightly apart and your tongue resting loosely in the base of your mouth.

This gentle wave of comfort then flows back down into your neck and shoulders and down through the arms.

Then the relaxation flows into the muscles of the upper arms, through the elbows, through the wrists, into the hands and fingers, right to the very ends of your fingertips.

Finally, take time to enjoy these wonderful feelings of relaxation throughout your entire body. Enjoy these feelings for as long as you want, and when you are ready, gently open your eyes and return to the present moment.

GUIDED IMAGERY OR VISUALISATION TECHNIQUES

As we mentioned earlier, some people relax through visual means rather than other means. Are you able to picture things in your mind? Try the following exercise to find out whether you can tap into visual means of relaxing.

VISUALISATION EXERCISE 1

Gently close your eyes and imagine that you are walking down a street that is familiar and safe to you. On that street

there are some parked cars, trees, houses and maybe some
other people out walking. Take a few moments to do this,
and then open your eyes.

Before reading on, write down whether you felt
visualising was easy or not so easy.

_____

_____

_____

_____

_____

_____

_____

_____

_____

Now answer these questions: What could you see or sense?
Were there some trees and if so what did they look like?
What colour were the cars?

_____

_____

_____

_____

_____

_____

_____

_____

Were you able to answer these questions? Did your answers surprise you? Most people can visualise a little bit, even if this involves just getting a sense of things around them. As mentioned above, some people find they are more 'auditory' (they relax with sounds, such as music) or 'kinesthetic' (they relax with movement such as walking), and will prefer other forms of relaxation to visual techniques. On the other hand, we find that a good visualisation technique also incorporates the five senses (sight, sound, touch, smell and taste) in the imagery to really engage your mind and body in a very relaxing experience.

A simple visualisation technique involves thinking of a safe and special place that you associate with peace and relaxation. It could be relaxing in the bath by candlelight with a good book, or walking along the beach on a stunningly beautiful day.

VISUALISATION EXERCISE 2
Make yourself comfortable (using the guidelines listed under 'Preparation for relaxation' on page 72), and imagine doing what you enjoy the most. Connect with that experience with all your senses. For example, in the bath you can see the flicker of the candle flames, you may smell the scent of the bubble bath, perhaps you can hear some soft, relaxing music in the background, you can feel the warmth of the water covering your whole body and finally you may have a sip of the refreshing drink that you have put by the side of the bath. Or if visualising the beach, notice the blue sky, the fluffy clouds, a gentle breeze, the warmth of the sun and sand, and the smell of the ocean. Are there others at the beach or are you alone? Are there sailing boats? Do you want to sit and enjoy what you can see, or do you want to walk or gather up shells?

Don't be concerned if you can't visualise very well. You may like to focus on one of your other senses that you relate to better. For example, you may like to listen to some music that you associate with relaxation, or you may simply want to focus on feeling a deepening sense of relaxation and comfort in your body. When you are ready to finish the form of relaxation you have chosen, gradually re-orient yourself to the present moment by being aware of the sounds around you, gently opening your eyes and looking around, and moving your body (for example, having a stretch).

MINDFULNESS RELAXATION TECHNIQUE

Mindfulness means paying attention in a particular way. It means taking notice of things, paying attention on purpose, non-judgementally and in the present moment. In other words, mindfulness refers to focusing on what you are doing and experiencing in the present moment.[2,3] For example, if you are brushing your teeth you are fully aware of and involved in every facet of the act of brushing your teeth. Or, if you are washing the dishes, take notice of the warmth of the water, the suds, the shiny surface of the clean dishes.

It has been suggested that feelings of depression are often associated with thinking about the past; for example, 'I feel sad that I did not finish high school.' In addition, anxiety is often associated with 'what if' thoughts about the future: 'What if I lose my job and can't pay the mortgage?' Mindfulness reminds us that the only moment we have any control over is the present one. You can, for example, only breathe one breath at a time.

It may be useful to try several short mindfulness exercises to help your understanding of this concept. For the first one, you will need a small piece of food, such as a strawberry. If you don't like strawberries (or have an allergy to strawberries), use what is available to you that you enjoy or can eat.

MINDFULNESS EXERCISE 1

Before you eat your piece of food, take time to study it using your senses other than taste; that is, take time to look at it, feel it, smell it and listen to it. What does it look like? Smell like? What is its texture? Now, place the piece of food into your mouth – roll it around slowly and explore it with your tongue. What does it feel like? Now slowly chew it. Is this noisy or quiet? What does it taste like? Is it crunchy or soft?

Write your discoveries on the lines below.

_____

_____

_____

_____

_____

Were you surprised that the strawberry smelled so strong, and that it sounded quite loud when you chewed it? Were you surprised at how crunchy the strawberry felt in your mouth? How is it that you had never noticed these things before? It is quite likely that your mind was thinking of something else instead of being mindful of you eating the strawberry.

MINDFULNESS EXERCISE 2

Another simple mindfulness exercise is to notice three things that you can see around you. Then notice three things that you can hear, and three things that you can feel or touch.

Again, try this exercise and jot down what you notice.

We will now take you through a longer mindfulness exercise. Take your time with each step of the meditation.

MINDFULNESS EXERCISE 3

Make yourself comfortable in a sitting relaxation position and let your eyes close. Notice the chair underneath you, supporting you, and notice the feel of your feet on the floor and your hands on your lap. Be aware of your breath, of the feel of the air as you breathe in and out, of breathing into the base of your lungs, using your diaphragm. Feel your abdomen rise and fall. Relax with each breath out. Be aware of the body, of feelings of relaxation flowing from the feet upwards through the body, up through the legs, the back, the chest, the head and neck and down into the arms. Notice how the body feels as you relax, as sometimes it can feel a bit lighter or heavier. Sometimes you feel that

you could not move it even if you wanted to. Now notice the sounds around you. Some are closer and some are further away. Focus on the sounds further away for a few moments. Now focus on the sounds closer to you. What can you hear?

Again bring your awareness to the chair underneath you, the feel of your feet and hands. Have a gentle stretch and, when you are ready, let your eyes open and be back in the room. Notice what is around you.

Some individuals like to make a recording for themselves of scripts such as the ones provided in the exercises in this chapter. Alternatively, we have recorded a relaxation CD of useful techniques to help relieve stress and anxiety for our clients and readers (see 'Further resources' later in this book).

Troubleshooting road blocks

Some common questions about relaxation are answered below, with the aim of reducing road blocks or barriers to you trying out the techniques on a regular basis.

Q: WHAT DO I DO WHEN I'M TOO TENSE TO RELAX?

A: Sometimes when people have been stressed for a long time they forget what it feels like to relax. There may be many different thoughts and feelings that make it difficult for the person to 'let go' of the tension they are holding. For example, some people associate the word relaxation with laziness and fear they will become a non-achiever if they stop striving constantly. For some people who are pushed around by these ideas it is easier to start with some form of active or physical relaxation; for example, a jog or a bike ride. The feeling of exhaustion at the end of a particularly strenuous workout is very much like the relaxation response.

Q: WHAT DO I DO WHEN I DON'T LIKE THE FEELINGS OF RELAXATION?

A: People tend to be creatures of habit and we are often uncomfortable with change and new sensations. However, there are many things that we have to do even when we don't feel like it. For example, many people don't particularly feel like going to the dentist, but they do because they know it is important for their health. Just like any new skill or sensation, relaxation will take a bit of time to get used to before you will begin to appreciate both the short-term and long-term benefits.

Perseverance is important at the start of learning any new skill. It is okay to set yourself a reasonable time limit or date to review your progress. You may choose to practise one relaxation technique daily for one month, and then review whether that particular technique is working for you. You will find a range of different types of relaxation methods to choose from throughout this chapter.

Q: WHAT IF I CAN'T FIND THE TIME TO RELAX?

A: Most people have picked up this book so they can feel less stressed and may be quite horrified to find that we are asking them to squeeze more tasks into their already overburdened day. It may be useful to view relaxation training as a good investment in time, both in the immediate and long-term future. Have you ever had so many things to do that you go from one job to another without being able to focus enough to adequately finish a single task? This is probably because your attention is scattered and split into too many different directions at the same time. Relaxation can help people focus that attention in one particular direction.

A useful analogy is how a magnifying glass can be used to focus the sun's rays in order to burn a leaf. Without the magnifying glass the power of the sun's rays is diluted – on their own, the rays do not have the power to burn the leaf. Theoretically, if you invest 20 minutes per day in relaxation training, you may find that your increased ability to focus your attention makes you so effective and efficient in completing your daily tasks that you may actually end up gaining more free time to do the things you really value.

Q: I AM WORRIED THAT IT WON'T WORK IF I DON'T HAVE 30 MINUTES OF RELAXATION EACH DAY.
A: It can be useful to initially set aside 20 or 30 minutes when you are trying to learn a relaxation technique. As you become more familiar with the techniques you tend to relax more readily and less time is needed. However, don't let time be an excuse – even 5 minutes of relaxation is useful. In fact, 'spot relaxations' are designed for very busy people who need to relax 'on the spot', which may be their desk at work, on the bus or at the kitchen sink at home!

Q: WHY DO I KEEP FALLING ASLEEP WHEN I RELAX?
A: Some people like to practise their relaxation at the end of the day lying in bed before they go to sleep. Naturally, there is going to be a strong likelihood that you will fall asleep when relaxing in this way. There is no problem with falling asleep when you relax, unless you are relaxing in a place where sleep is not appropriate, such as your desk at work. If you do not want to fall asleep it may be useful to practise your relaxation

in the sitting position and at a time of day when you tend to be more alert.

Q: I FEEL TOO GUILTY TO RELAX DURING THE DAY WHEN MY CHILDREN ARE HOME, AND AT NIGHT I AM TOO TIRED. WHAT SHOULD I DO?

A: Ask yourself the following question: If I had to go to hospital today (for any reason) who would look after my children? Would these people do as good a job as you? Probably not. People often get strong messages about what is expected of them from a very young age. Many women are trained into being 'people pleasers'. That is, they are given not-so-subtle messages that a nice person puts other people's needs first, otherwise she may be labelled as selfish. This can become problematic as the woman has children and slowly gains more and more people that she is responsible for taking care of. As her list of responsibilities gets longer she often comes at the bottom of the list of priorities with little or no time to spend on her own self-care. It can often take some kind of crisis before the person realises that they cannot keep taking care of others unless they prioritise their own self-care. Consequently, it makes sense to put yourself at the top of your priorities list and invest in your own relaxation practice, as it is not only the best thing for you but it will also ensure that you are in a fit state to care for those you love.

Q: I HAVE LIVED THIS LONG WITHOUT RELAXING, WHY SHOULD I START NOW?

A: In Chapter 1, we discussed how stress and anxiety may have a cumulative effect over many years. Often when people come to see us they are trying to understand why they are experiencing stress or anxiety at this particular point in time.

When a farmer grows a crop for many years on the one field, the crop will decline in quality each year. The farmer must rest the field and replenish the soil periodically. Similarly, relaxation is a way of nurturing and replenishing our minds and bodies so that we can continue to grow and flourish. We have also emphasised, in this chapter, the importance of relaxation as a preventative measure in keeping our stress at a manageable level.

Q: HOW DO I KNOW I AM BENEFITING FROM RELAXATION?

A: Anyone can learn to relax and experience some benefits. Relaxation techniques can provide quick and simple ways to gain a sense of control and mastery when we are feeling overwhelmed by stress. In this way they can also make us feel a bit better and not judge ourselves so harshly. There are many mental and physical benefits from relaxing, including decreased blood pressure, breathing rate, muscle tension, sweating, adrenaline flow and lowered mental arousal.

Q: I CAN'T STOP MYSELF THINKING?

A: For people who have very busy minds it may be useful to have a relaxation CD incorporating guided imagery. Preferably, the guided imagery used should encompass your five senses and be complex enough to keep your busy mind totally engaged in the experience. However, if you feel your mind wandering don't be concerned. This is completely normal and happens to most people. When you become aware that you have been distracted, the key is to let your thoughts drift by and return to listening to the voice on the CD. It can be counterproductive to try too hard to concentrate on the CD because this type of earnestness will probably cause muscle tension and negative thinking. So we suggest accepting that your mind will wander at times, and that you can simply refocus your attention on the relaxation when it does.

Relaxation training form

It can be helpful when you are first starting relaxation practice to keep a record of your progress. This can help to keep you accountable, and can also be very reinforcing of your efforts as you see your self-estimated level of stress begin to go down. The record in Table 7 is a sample and is very simple to fill out. Each time you practise you write in the date, how long the relaxation was in minutes, your estimate of your stress level before the relaxation and then after the relaxation. Then finally you add any comments that may be useful to you for future practice, or which you might like to discuss with your mental health professional. The scale to measure your stress level is the same as discussed in Chapter 2, where 0 = no stress, and 10 = the most stress you have ever experienced.

TABLE 7: RELAXATION TRAINING PROGRESS FORM

Date	Time taken	Stress level before	Stress level after	Comments
25/9/09	15 mins	10	8	Felt better – progressive muscle relaxation
26/9/09	25 mins	8	5	Guided imagery – got interrupted
27/9/09	20 mins	9	6	Mindfulness technique – really liked it

Other types of relaxation

Relaxation strategies do not need to be new, complex or time-consuming. Below are some relaxation ideas you may like to experiment with.

- Reading a book or watching a movie.
- Simple stretches that can help loosen tight areas.
- Having a bath or massage.
- Taking a walk somewhere with nice scenery.
- Listening to or playing music.
- Having a cup of tea or coffee with a friend.
- Engaging in a hobby such as painting, gardening or photography.
- Yoga, tai chi, hypnosis.

ON THE LINES BELOW WRITE DOWN WHAT ACTIVITIES YOU FIND RELAXING.

_____

_____

_____

_____

_____

_____

Back to balance

Balance is not a 'black and white' concept, of either having total balance or not having any balance at all. Balance generally refers to a state in which two opposing forces are in equilibrium.

However, in life the system is often more complex and there will be more than two opposing forces, and a sense of balance or equilibrium is required for the system to work. We can aim to make adjustments so the system is more stable and there is a greater sense of equilibrium.[4] In this section we will look at balance between stress and relaxation in the first instance, and then consider balance in the broader 'system' or domains in life.

Balance can mean getting the right amount of relaxation and stress in your life. These amounts will be different for different people, and it is important to remember that stress is not always a bad thing. There are in fact some positive effects of stress. As we saw with the fight or flight response, stress can help you stay safe and perform well. In fact, the exact same stress response happens in our body when we are frightened by an oncoming car or win the lottery – the only difference is how we think about these two events. We will talk more about thinking in Chapter 4.

Everyone has a level of stress that is adaptive or helpful. It is important to determine what a comfortable level of stress is for you. Interestingly, in his book *The Stress of Life*, Hans Selye suggested that distress is experienced when someone has nothing worthwhile to do (not enough stress) or when they are overtaxed by constant activity (too much stress).[5] Can you relate different times in your life to either of these? Also, Yerkes and Dodson put forward a useful model to try to understand how to find your stress comfort zone. They proposed that as stress increases so do performance and wellbeing until the stress comfort zone is achieved.[6] The diagram opposite, known as the Yerkes-Dodson curve, depicts the relationship between stress and performance. At the start of the stress comfort zone, extra stress is handled easily but as the individual moves towards overstimulation or too much stress, performance diminishes markedly.

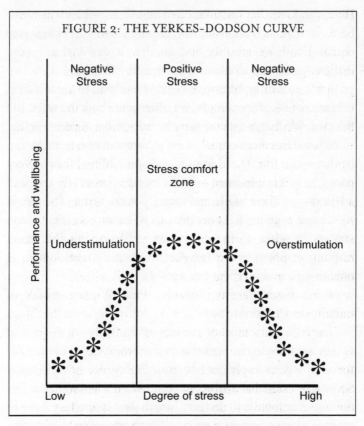

FIGURE 2: THE YERKES-DODSON CURVE

Negative Stress | Positive Stress | Negative Stress

Performance and wellbeing

Stress comfort zone

Understimulation

Overstimulation

Low | Degree of stress | High

Source: Browne, W. 1986, *Learn to Unwind: A workbook on relaxation and stress management techniques*, Health Media and Education Centre.

This model emphasises the importance of clarifying the correct level of stress for you. Sometimes it is necessary to have brief and purposeful periods of overstimulation, such as when a family member is sick or an important project at work is due. However, a realistic goal would be to spend the majority of your time in the stress comfort zone. Many people get tricked into an overstressed lifestyle because they push themselves into the overstimulation/negative stress zone for periods of time, thinking that once that demand is met they will move back into their stress comfort zone. However, when one demand follows another and another it can make it very difficult to sustain a balanced and healthy lifestyle.

In life generally, balance can also be related to the different domains of life; for example, we often hear about the work-life balance. We like to view it more broadly and consider whether there is balance between all of the different domains, including health, work, family and friends, and spirituality. It can be very tricky to achieve balance – it is a bit like a butterfly that will settle on you for a while and then fly away again. The aim is to achieve regular or longer periods of balance in life, to help achieve a sense of harmony and wellbeing. In this state, nothing in life is out of proportion, and no one domain is emphasised at the expense of another.

In his book *Perfect Balance*, Paul Wilson speaks of imbalance occurring when there is conflict between the things we have to do, should do, things others want us to do, and things we want to do. Sometimes our own ideas, ambitions or work practices contribute to imbalance. We have already spoken of individuals who put their own needs last in life. As the list of responsibilities gets longer they often have little or no time to spend on their own self-care, including relaxation.[7]

How do you think this might lead to imbalance?

_____

_____

_____

_____

_____

Society itself can influence some of these ideas, ambitions and practices. Consider the following question: If you imagine yourself growing up under the 'umbrella' of society, what things will influence you and your ideas?

_____

_____

_____

_____

_____

_____

We suggest that many things will influence you and your ideas, including family, peers, school and other educational institutions, culture, religion, the media and government. It is worth considering what ideas males and females develop in our society – the male as the fit and strong breadwinner, and the woman as the nurturer, mother and worker. Do you think these ideas might influence what we think and do in life, and how we set our priorities? How might consumerism in our society push us to focus on one area at the expense of others, for example? If we focus on particular domains in life, and ignore others, tension and ill-health may result.

We need motivation to change and to restore a sense of balance. A place to start is to review the different domains in life (as we have done earlier in Chapter 2), as this will enable you to know exactly where you are right now. We are going to suggest some other ways to restore balance in the next few exercises.

EGGS IN THE BASKET EXERCISE

You have probably heard the saying 'Don't put all your eggs in one basket'. This saying is suggesting it is better to put a few eggs in several baskets thereby lessening the chance of losing all your eggs if there is an accident. We are going to use this idea to take you through an exercise that will help you visualise how many baskets your 'time and energy eggs' are going into, and whether your time and energy is being spread in a balanced way over the nine value domains we discussed in Chapter 2.This exercise is based on a similar exercise used by Dr Ailsa Burns.[8]

As you can see in Figure 3, you have nine baskets labelled with the value domains such as family and friends, work and leisure. You also have 27 eggs which symbolise all your time and energy. For the first part of this exercise we would like you to place in each basket the number of eggs that represents how much time and energy you are putting into that particular value domain at the present time. For example, you may have nine eggs in the work domain, nine in the family domain, five in the leisure domain, four in the health domain, and none in the remaining domains. Your eggs should add up to 27.

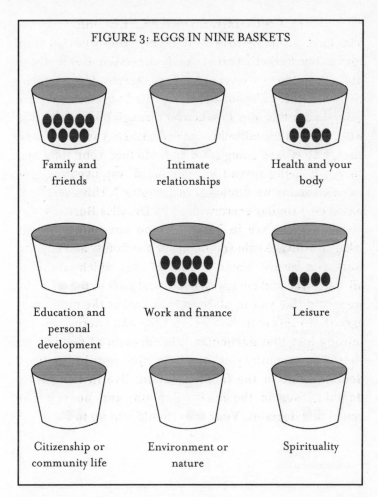

FIGURE 3: EGGS IN NINE BASKETS

Family and
friends

Intimate
relationships

Health and your
body

Education and
personal
development

Work and finance

Leisure

Citizenship or
community life

Environment or
nature

Spirituality

The next part of the exercise involves you redistributing your eggs to represent how you would like your eggs to be distributed. For example, in a perfect world to have a perfectly balanced life you may strive to have three eggs in every domain basket. However, if there is a domain you don't particularly relate to, you could try to evenly distribute your eggs between the remaining baskets.

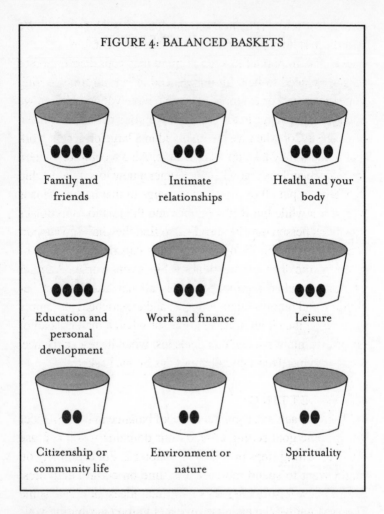

FIGURE 4: BALANCED BASKETS

Family and friends

Intimate relationships

Health and your body

Education and personal development

Work and finance

Leisure

Citizenship or community life

Environment or nature

Spirituality

Now it is time to reflect on the differences in the distribution of your eggs at the present time versus what you would prefer the distribution to be like. You might like to draw these distributions out on the 'Travel diary' page at the end of this chapter. This is also an opportunity to think about how you might get more eggs into a certain basket, such as family, or how to get fewer eggs in a certain domain, such as work. We will discuss how you might do this in a moment.

It is also important to keep in mind that your distribution of eggs may need to be a bit unbalanced at certain times during your life span. For example, when we have young children we may need more eggs in the family basket for a period of time out of necessity, or when we are involved in a large project at work that domain may take up a lot of time. Also a common pattern for many people is that when they enter a new love relationship they tend to put all or most of their eggs in that basket. This is okay for a while but if it continues and the relationship breaks down that person may be surprised to find they have no support available from family or friends. This can make the pain of grieving the loss of the relationship even worse. Another example is when a woman focuses all her attention on her children and ignores other domains, and experiences an 'empty nest' when the children leave home, or when a man puts all of his efforts into work and then feels lost when he retires. Hence, the old saying 'Don't put all your eggs in one basket'.

GOAL SETTING

To help you achieve a greater sense of balance in life, consider doing some goal setting around your domains – you can use the goal-setting steps provided in Chapter 2. For example, you might want to spend more or less time on certain activities, explore new leisure interests or spiritual ideas, or create some clearer boundaries between work and home (for example, no work at home).[9] You will need to continually review these ideas and goals over time and make small changes to maintain a sense of balance as life moves on. This is part of the challenge, but also part of the fun!

We would like to share a relaxation technique which is based on the idea of three buckets, and which relates to some of the domains and the idea of balance. Read the exercise below and see if you think it will be useful for you.

THREE BUCKETS EXERCISE

Make yourself comfortable and let your eyes close. We would like you to imagine three buckets with lids, sitting on a shelf. Notice the size and colours of the buckets. The first bucket represents everything to do with you and your life – your dreams and goals, ideas and interests. The second bucket represents other people, and everything to do with them. The third bucket represents the world we live in, the social codes we live by (laws, government policies, morals) and the environment.

Lift the lid off the first bucket and take a look inside. You can spend a lot of time dealing with everything in this bucket and you can influence it greatly. You can add and remove things from this bucket.

Now have a look in the second bucket, to do with other people. You can influence this bucket to some degree, by helping or hindering, but you have less control over this bucket because you cannot control other people. Sometimes you need to put the lid on this bucket and put it back on the shelf.

Now explore the third bucket. Again, you can add to this bucket by getting involved with your community or helping the environment, but there may be limits to what you can do.

We can become very stressed about the buckets to do with others and our world, when there are actually limitations on how much influence we can have on these buckets. Sometimes we need to focus on our own bucket and put the others aside for a while.

When you are ready, open your eyes and come back to the room. How did you find this exercise? What did you think it meant?

_____

_____

_____

_____

_____

In our experience, individuals can become very stressed about issues with family, friends, or the world around them. Sometimes we need to place limits on what we worry about and put the worries away for a while. It can be useful to recognise the things that you have more control over, and those that you have little influence over. It is not helpful to get hooked into worrying too much about other people's problems or world crises such as earthquakes or starving children. Worrying will not help you or them. However, you can choose to do something practical to help, such as making a donation or sponsoring a child. Once you have taken this action, you need to let go of the worry. What we can then do is come back to ourselves and work on our own ways of dealing with stress.

Healthy lifestyle

Last but not least we are going to focus on achieving a healthy lifestyle. This refers to managing stress and also incorporating healthy eating, exercise and good sleep into your life. We will focus on nutrition, exercise and sleep in this section as they form the cornerstone to achieving a sense of balance in life.

NUTRITION

We need a healthy intake of food to provide energy and to allow the body to function and repair itself. When stressed, eating can be the last thing (we undereat) or the main thing (we overeat) on our minds. However, it is vital not to neglect or abuse the body when we are stressed or anxious – in fact, healthy eating is probably the first step in managing these problems.

A healthy nutritional intake refers to eating all the essential nutrients in adequate amounts for good health and avoiding excess nutrients that might contribute to ill-health.[10] It also refers to enjoying a wide range of foods, including plenty of fresh colourful foods such as vegetables and fruit, quality protein foods (lean meat, fish, poultry, legumes, nuts), cereals and dairy foods.

The old adage of 'eating in moderation' still applies, especially to fats, sugars, salt and alcohol. The literature suggests that we should aim to eat mono-unsaturated fats (such as olive oil) rather than saturated (solid) fats, and reduced-fat dairy foods. Foods that have a low glycaemic index (those that raise sugar levels the least) such as wholegrain breads and legumes are healthier than those with a high glycaemic index (such as cakes, lollies, white bread and other refined carbohydrates).

The most important meal of the day is breakfast as it will give you the energy to get through busy mornings. We suggest having a decent breakfast each day, maybe cereals (preferably wholegrain) and a serve of protein (such as an egg or some low-fat cheese). These foods will keep you satisfied and energised for a good length of time.

Fish oils have been suggested as being beneficial for brain function, and also magnesium, which has been recommended for use during periods of prolonged stress and to aid sleep. Magnesium is found in some nuts and fish, eggs, wholegrain cereals and mineral water, or can be taken as a supplement.[11]

The majority of our body is made up of water. It is vital to every cell in the body, and it is reported that adults should drink about 2 litres a day.[12] This might include green tea (which is high in anti-oxidants, and contains L-theanine), with recent research suggesting that it may be helpful for our general health and in stress/anxiety.[13] It is best to reduce caffeinated drinks as these tend to be dehydrating.

When we are stressed or anxious, we tend to reach for caffeinated drinks, wine, or sugary or fatty foods such as chocolate. This is because stress and anxiety use up a lot of energy and tend to tire us out. However, eating simple sugars such as lollies or drinking caffeinated drinks such as coffee or energy drinks can be a problem. They place extra demands on the body – with sweet foods our body has to produce a surge of insulin from the pancreas to deal with the rush of sugar, and caffeinated drinks cause our heart rate to rise. You may feel better in the short term, but not very good after a little while.

Another approach is to notice when these behaviours occur (for example, between 4 p.m. and 5 p.m. each day), and then aim to prevent them or to be prepared! Eat a healthy breakfast and lunch, and have a mid-afternoon snack, such as fruit or cheese and biscuits, to keep you satisfied later in the day. Other strategies which may assist in dealing with these cravings include:

- delay – do something until the urge passes; for example, go for a walk or read a book
- have small, regular meals (five or six a day)
- have a warm, healthy drink
- do some relaxation – especially breathing techniques.

Jot down ideas that might be helpful to you for healthier eating.

_____

_____

_____

_____

_____

MELISSA'S STORY

Melissa joined the military as an officer working in the health area. Early on in her training she was faced with passing a fitness test which involved running 5 kilometres in thirteen minutes! She had not played sport for a long time and her fitness was right down.

Melissa decided to talk with a fitness trainer, who encouraged her to set a goal and gradually work towards it. Running the 5 kilometres in the given time became the six-week goal. She began with a first week goal of walking 50 metres, then running 50 metres, and repeating this for a few laps of the oval. The fitness instructor also advised Melissa to write down the distance she ran every day, and to check her time once a week.

After a week the first step was achieved, and each subsequent week Melissa's distance and time running were increased. By six weeks, Melissa passed her 5-kilometre run in twelve minutes to her own amazement! Setting a goal and breaking it down into small steps really worked, and having a written record of the steps and progress also helped Melissa.

EXERCISE

It is well established that exercise has a positive effect on mood, results in increased physical fitness, promotes a sense of wellbeing and aids sleep. Various reasons for these effects have been suggested such as an increased release of endorphins (natural morphine-like substances) or neurotransmitters (chemicals carrying messages between nerves) in the brain. Other mechanisms include the reduction of muscle tension and the induction of a meditative state.[14]

What exercise do you enjoy? Do you like walking, tennis, squash, going to the gym, netball or yoga? Walking in a lovely place such as the beach or the countryside can be especially relaxing. Is exercise a regular part of your week, or is it worth setting a goal around getting started with some exercise?

Now consider Melissa's story, and see how she set her goal and worked towards it gradually.

What are your fitness goals? Jot them down here, making sure that they are realistic and achievable. Also, be specific and set a time frame to achieve them by.

_____

_____

_____

_____

_____

_____

_____

_____

Remember that there are a few safeguards with exercise – if you are going to undertake strenuous exercise and are concerned about health conditions, then consult your GP for advice. You might want to do some gentle stretches beforehand, especially if you are not used to exercise. And always start with a small amount of exercise and build up slowly. You will be surprised how you gain fitness when you are persistent and build up your efforts.

MINIMISING DRUGS AND ALCOHOL
Remember that many drugs will heighten anxiety, including caffeine in coffee, nicotine in cigarettes or amphetamines. We often hear from individuals that they feel particularly anxious and are not sure why, but on more direct questioning we find that they are smoking 30 cigarettes a day, or drinking twelve cups of coffee a day. It is important to reduce the impact of drugs on your anxiety symptoms by minimising drug use. Help can be sought from your GP, therapist or various community agencies.

SLEEP
Sleep is another vital element to health, and it is often disturbed when we are stressed or anxious. It may be that we cannot get off to sleep because we are worrying about a number of things and cannot calm the mind, or we may be wakeful during the night or awake early in the morning. To work out what is happening with your sleep it may be worthwhile keeping a sleep diary, such as the one below. It should be kept over 24 hours, for several days to a week.

TABLE 8: SLEEP DIARY

Time of day	Activity	Sleep
7am		Awake
10am	Shopping	
12 midday	Lunch	
2pm	Gardening	
3pm		Short nap
7pm	Dinner	
10pm	Go to bed	Unable to sleep
12 midnight	Toilet	Got to sleep
3am		Could not sleep as thinking of lots of things
4am		Got to sleep
7am		Awake

Once you have a picture of your sleeping patterns, you can then more easily work on the troubles that you are having with sleep, such as difficulty getting off to sleep. Think about what has helped before, such as having a warm milky drink or a relaxing bath in the evening, or perhaps writing down your thoughts before you go to sleep. Other sleep tips include:

- Try not to worry about not being able to sleep; instead be mindful of your breath.
- Establish a sleep routine, so that you go to bed about the same time each night, and have a wind-down routine before going to bed, such as having a warm drink before cleaning your teeth.

- Use your relaxation techniques in bed at night or perhaps listen to a relaxation CD.
- Avoid caffeine from mid-afternoon, and avoid overeating at night.
- Ensure that your room is comfortable and relaxing, in terms of noise, lighting and temperature.
- Exercise during the day (again, not too late in the day) will cause you to be more physically tired at night.
- Avoid stimulating television or reading before bed.
- Lavender or hop-and-lavender pillows are mildly sedating (but beware of sensitivities to these substances and they should not be used if pregnant).
- If still struggling to get to sleep after half an hour, consider getting up and repeating your regular wind down or doing something boring such as ironing.

Relaxation techniques which may be particularly helpful at night include breathing and progressive muscle relaxation. Counting backwards from 200 can focus your mind and stop you thinking about worrying thoughts. Also, particular visual imagery can be helpful, such as imagining a whiteboard in your mind. In one corner, carefully write the number one, then in the centre slowly write a word to do with sleep, then rub these off slowly. In another corner write the number two, and in the centre, write another word to do with sleep, then rub off and keep going with subsequent numbers.[15]

TRAVEL REMINDERS
Here are some reminders from this chapter. You may want to copy them and make them into a reminder card to place in your diary or wallet, or even on the fridge or a mirror at home.

- Stress is a response to a demand, and the fight or flight response can occur in stress or anxiety.
- The stress bucket is a metaphor to illustrate how stress can build up and 'spill over'.
- The opposite to stress is relaxation, and this can be used to prevent or reduce stress.
- There is a range of relaxation techniques including breathing, muscle relaxation, visualisation and mindfulness.
- Balance refers to achieving the right amount of stress and relaxation in your life. A healthy lifestyle can assist.

TRAVEL DIARY

THE TRICKS AND TRAPS OF STRESS AND ANXIETY

To get through the hardest journey we only need to take one step at a time, but we must keep on stepping.

—Chinese proverb

Learning new things can be hard. Making a decision to change can be very confronting and exciting at the same time. You have probably tried many different ways to deal with your feelings and thoughts of stress and anxiety. It can be frustrating to try the same strategy over and over again, expecting, but not achieving, a different outcome. Sometimes trying something new and different feels like cutting a pathway with a machete through the very dense undergrowth of a jungle, whereas reverting to old habits feels like strolling down a well-worn path that is clear and easy. That is why we sometimes stick with the old habits.

However, the problem with the old and well-worn path is that it does not take you to a fulfilling and valued destination, but back to the same old place where you think, feel and do the same old things. Because going down this path is automatic, easy and familiar, it seems as if you are sometimes halfway there before you even know it!

New behaviours can result in a new pathway through your brain as well. As highlighted earlier, recent research has indicated that our brains are quite malleable and capable of change. This is great news as it means we are never too old or too set in our ways to change. In this chapter we are going to uncover how stress and anxiety have been tricking and trapping you into certain thoughts and behaviours that do not fit with what you want for your life. First of all we will address some of the common myths about anxiety, and then we will focus on some of the ways our minds throw unhelpful thoughts our way and why this happens.

Common myths about anxiety

MYTH 1: LABELLING IS HELPFUL

Labelling can be enticing. It tricks you into thinking that knowing more about your problem will lead to knowing a way out or a solution. It is important to ask yourself whether knowing a lot about anxiety disorders and finding a label that fits what you are feeling has been helpful. It has probably provided you with some comfort to know you are not alone and others experience the same thing. However, some of the clients we see have fallen into the trap of buying into the label of their 'disorder'. You can be tricked into becoming the 'disorder', thinking and behaving like someone with an anxiety disorder.

Anxiety does not totalise you as a person – it's just one part in the bigger picture of your life. It does not speak of your identity. It is very important to see the anxiety as the problem and to separate it from you, the person. As mentioned earlier, in narrative therapy a great emphasis is placed on separating the person's identity from the anxiety for which they seek assistance. This is based on the idea that the problem is the problem, as opposed to the person being seen as the problem.[1]

MYTH 2: ANXIETY PROBLEMS ARE IN THE MAIN HEREDITARY

Research suggests the genetic contribution to anxiety disorders is about 30 to 40 per cent.[2] Therefore a person may inherit an anxious predisposition, but this is different from inheriting an anxiety disorder. The good news is the other 60 to 70 per cent has to do with how you deal with anxious thoughts and feelings. This is something you can change to live the life you want.

MYTH 3: HAPPINESS IS NORMAL

Our culture supports the idea that happiness is a constant state of mind for humans. However, there are many problems in life that will cause emotional pain, including death, illness, work stress, divorce and accidents. Also, statistics indicate that one in five adults will experience depression. These facts highlight that it would not be natural for happiness to be a constant state of being, especially when we have just experienced a loss or trauma.

However, happiness can occur frequently and is often a spontaneous feeling. The trick is that we might not take the time to be mindful of it and enjoy it fully when it happens. Many people believe everyone else is happy except themselves, which is actually not the case and again may lead to unhappiness.

MYTH 4: ANXIETY IS A SIGN OF WEAKNESS

The fourth myth follows on from the third one. Our society assumes that psychological suffering is defective or abnormal, and it is depicted as a disorder, illness or weakness and a result of a mind that is somehow defective or faulty.[3] Consequently, when we experience suffering due to our thoughts and feelings we label ourselves as weak or stupid or abnormal.

This myth is supported by two sources, the first of which we call the 'snapshot'. This is our tendency to take a quick look at other people's lives, a bit like a two-dimensional photo, and then make many assumptions based on the very limited information given by that picture. When you see others for a small period of time, you may not see them as anxious or stressed. You may have thought, 'Why can't I be happy like them?' You might then jump to the conclusion, 'Something's wrong with me. I am weak, broken, hopeless . . .' However, what is needed is a change of perspective. If you were able to have more of a movie of this person's life, rather than a snapshot, you would see for yourself that they are just like you, and experience the spectrum of good and bad feelings as you do.

The second source that fuels the weakness myth is social comparison. If you view everyone else as having it easy and being happy but see your own life narrowly, as being all about anxiety, then you will tend to think that they have something you don't have. If you continue to believe your anxiety stems from some kind of character flaw, broken part or inherent weakness then you will remain stuck.[4]

The CBT model

Having read through these myths about anxiety, you will have been aware that the discussion focused on thoughts and feelings, and how sometimes thoughts can lead to uncomfortable feelings. This is a view encapsulated in the CBT model which was introduced in Chapter 2. The CBT model is shown opposite in Figure 5, and we will explain it in detail in this chapter.

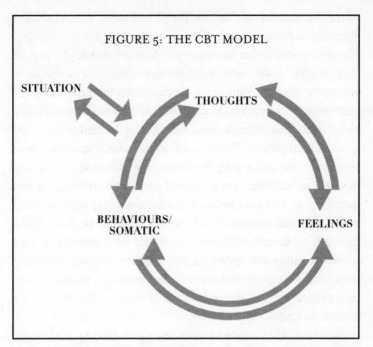

FIGURE 5: THE CBT MODEL

SITUATION

THOUGHTS

BEHAVIOURS/
SOMATIC

FEELINGS

Source: Adapted from Greenberger, D. and Padesky, C. 1995, *Mind Over Mood: Change how you feel by changing the way you think*, The Guildford Press, New York.

The CBT model is built on the premise that all of our thoughts, feelings and behaviour are interlinked and affect each other.[5] Consequently, our thoughts affect our feelings and our feelings affect our thoughts. Our feelings affect our behaviour and our behaviour affects our feelings. Finally, our thoughts affect our behaviour and our behaviour has an impact on our thoughts. You can see in the diagram how the arrows all go in two directions, showing these relationships.

This interrelationship also means that at times a vicious cycle can be set up, whereby anxious thoughts trigger anxious feelings (or vice versa), which in turn trigger more anxious thoughts. Have you ever had this experience? Panic episodes are a good example. The individual can notice a physical sensation, such as palpitations (or an increased heart rate), and they might think, 'Oh no, I'm going to have a panic attack.' The next thing is that another symptom arises and the person then thinks, 'My anxiety is getting worse.' The cycle is occurring and the symptoms and anxious thoughts feed off each other in a cascade, and worsen. We will talk specifically about dealing with panic episodes later (see Chapter 9).

We like to think of this model as representing each one of us. We all have thoughts, behaviours (which may include the physical or 'somatic' symptoms of stress and anxiety, such as sweating or shallow breathing) and feelings, and we have different situations or events in our lives. The diagram in Figure 5 illustrates this and where we can potentially take action or intervene to reduce our stress or anxiety – namely with our thoughts, behaviours, feelings or the situation. However, not all of these are equally easy or effective. Let's explore this idea a little bit more.

Sometimes we might need to problem-solve to modify the situation. For example, our workplace may be a source of stress, and we might need to consider making changes within the workplace, changes in how we react to it, or even changing workplaces. (See Chapter 5 for further information on problem-solving.) Next, let's consider our behaviours, and to begin with we want you to try another exercise.

MODIFYING BEHAVIOUR EXERCISE
Carefully get up out of your chair and stand and stretch your arms out to the sides of your body if you are able. Describe your experience on the lines below.

_____

_____

How did you go? Was this pretty easy? This task is designed to illustrate that our behaviour is totally in our control (unless, of course, we have some physical disability). Therefore it makes sense when dealing with our stress to begin with behaviours over which we have a great deal of control, such as relaxation and lifestyle, before going onto other areas (such as thoughts and feelings) over which we may have less control. That is why we have already talked about some behavioural strategies that can help in Chapter 3, and we will return to others in the next chapter.

Let's look at feelings now, and we want you to try another exercise.

MODIFYING FEELINGS EXERCISE
Make yourself feel ecstatically happy. Write down your
experience on the lines below.

_____

_____

_____

_____

_____

We suspect this was not an easy task. If it was possible, you probably would not need to read this book! Actors manage this sort of task by thinking about and focusing on a situation in their lives when they were very happy. Even they find it difficult to tap directly into the feeling. The message is that we cannot control our feelings at will, and so in terms of the CBT model, it is more difficult to intervene directly at the feeling level.

However, that is not to say that expressing troublesome feelings such as worry cannot be helpful. For example, you might talk to a friend or therapist and express how you feel, or you might write down your feelings in a journal. Some individuals express their feelings through music or creative activities such as drawing or pottery.

What means might you use to express your feelings? Jot down your ideas here.

_____

_____

_____

_____

_____

_____

Another technique to help manage uncomfortable feelings comes from surfing! Have you been surfing or body-boarding? We are going to ask you to imagine a great day at the beach and if you like the water you can be out with a board. (If you don't like the water, then just imagine watching the wave riders.) There are some great waves. To ride a wave, you have to catch it first. You then move with the wave, just ahead of the peak of the wave. You can aim to do the same with anxious feelings: be aware, observe them or catch them early, stay just ahead of them by using your relaxation techniques or the cognitive ones you will learn in this chapter. Also notice that the wave finishes. Anxiety does not go on and on forever, it waxes and wanes, just like the wave.

We are now going to consider thoughts and have another few exercises for you to try.

MODIFYING THOUGHTS EXERCISE
We would like you to gently close your eyes and think about nothing. Just let your mind be an empty and clear space for ten seconds as you try to think about nothing. Describe your experience below.

_____

_____

_____

_____

_____

_____

How did you go? If you found it extremely difficult to think of nothing, congratulations! This was the aim of the exercise. Most people reveal that when they are trying to think of nothing in this exercise they are still thinking of something. Usually they are thinking about what they think nothing looks like, sounds like or feels like. The point from this exercise is that we are always thinking about something, and the issue is whether we are aware of those thoughts or not. CBT proposes that what we think affects how we feel and in turn affects what we do. Therefore, an important part of CBT involves becoming aware of what we are thinking and beginning to understand how that can make us feel and act.

UNDERSTANDING THOUGHTS EXERCISE
We would like you to gently close your eyes and imagine that you see a good friend walking down the road in the distance. You shout out your friend's name but he/she keeps on walking. How do you react? Describe your response on the lines below.

_____

_____

_____

_____

_____

_____

How did you describe your reaction? With a feeling (such as disappointment)? A thought ('Why didn't she see me, was she ignoring me?')? Or a behaviour? Over the many times we have completed this exercise we have found the majority of people describe their reaction using the following words: angry, sad, rejected, upset, frustrated, guilty, annoyed, neutral, relieved, happy. The range of responses leads us to ponder the question: 'How do we explain such an array of different responses to the same event?'

The CBT model and the Rational-Emotive Therapy model from which CBT draws can help us answer this question by using what is called the ABC analysis. The 'A' in the ABC analysis stands for the 'Activating Event'. In this case the activating event was seeing the friend walking down the street, calling out to the friend and the friend continuing to walk. The 'Consequences' or 'C' to this event were some feelings, perhaps sadness, anger or relief. So for us to move from the same 'A', the activating event, to the 'C', or consequence, which involves different feelings for different people, it would appear there is a step in between that defines the different outcomes.[6]

This between step is 'B', which stands for your beliefs, thoughts or perceptions. We can work out what the intervening thoughts were likely to be by looking at the event and the subsequent emotions. You saw your friend walking down the street, you shouted out their name and they kept on walking and you felt angry.

What kind of thoughts, beliefs, or perceptions would explain someone feeling angry in that situation? Write them on the lines below.

_____

_____

_____

_____

_____

What type of thoughts, beliefs, or perceptions would someone have to have about the exact same situation in order to have neutral feelings?

_____

_____

_____

_____

_____

Finally, what type of thoughts, beliefs, or perceptions would someone have to have to feel relieved about that exact same situation?

_____

_____

_____

_____

_____

_____

_____

To feel angry in the above situation a person may have thoughts such as, 'She is ignoring me on purpose! How dare she ignore me! This is just awful, terrible. Why is she doing this? What have I done wrong? I'll teach her to treat me like this.' For someone to feel neutral they may have had thoughts including, 'Maybe she didn't hear me. I didn't shout loud enough. Oh well, it doesn't matter . . . I'll catch up with her next time.' Finally, to feel relieved the person may have thought that their friend was in a hurry and might not have had time to talk anyway, but felt relieved they had made an attempt to be socially appropriate.

This exercise was developed to illustrate how humans are described as 'meaning-making' beings, as we are always trying to make sense of what is happening around us. Many people believe that the feelings and emotions they are experiencing are caused by someone else. They may also believe a certain situation or an external event causes their feelings. You may have heard people say, 'my boss stresses me out' or 'that job interview made me anxious'. Underlying these statements is the belief that someone or something is able to make us feel a certain way. In reality, no one can make us feel anything – it is the meaning we make, or the thoughts we have about the situation that stimulate our feelings.

Through this example we can really see how thinking influences feelings. Therefore, if we want to manage our feelings of anxiety and stress it would make sense to look at the types of unhelpful thinking that lead to painful feelings. Let's take the example of Tom.

TOM'S STORY

Tom is unhappy in his job. He moved to this position six months ago because it was a better job with more money, and he thought he would get greater job satisfaction. Tom has always been an 'anxious person' and he feels this has restricted his ascent up the corporate ladder. He believes all his colleagues have had it easier than him because they did not have to deal with the anxiety he experiences. He wants to enjoy his work as other people do but he is starting to think he will never find a job he likes. His current job involves managing a team of six people and reporting to the director of the company. Tom senses that his team members don't like him and three of his team members are after his job.

Due to this, he feels pressure to always perform perfectly to avoid any challenges to his management position. Tom's end-of-month report was criticised in front of the director and other clients. Now Tom thinks

---

he is a 'failure' and feels anxious entering the office because he thinks everyone is talking about his poor performance and is waiting for him to be fired. He worries that his company may lose some important clients because of his report and that a co-worker will use the incident to get his job. Tom is also concerned that he may never find another job and will not be able to pay the bills, including the mortgage. Tom has started worrying on Saturday night about going back to work on Monday. He is snappy with his children and has started to withdraw from social functions on the weekend, so he can do work at home.

Tom is struggling with worry. What is troubling him, and what traps do you think he is falling into with his thinking?

Unhelpful thinking tricks and traps

Tom's mind has certainly led him up the garden path with a myriad unhelpful thinking tricks and traps. We can see that Tom is falling into the trap of comparing himself to others and coming to the conclusion that he is not good enough and is different or damaged in some way. He also believes that he is the only one who experiences anxiety and others are happy all the time. He has been tricked into trying to be perfect as a way of managing the anxiety and the belief that if he just worked harder he would be able to stop feeling anxious. His mind is feeding him so many unhelpful thoughts and triggering so many painful feelings that he is overwhelmed and just wants to run away. This leaves us with the question: Why is Tom's mind being so unhelpful to him? The answer lies in the story of our evolution.

Evolution of the unhappy mind

The human mind did not evolve to make us feel good. Our minds evolved to ensure that we stayed alive in a world full of danger. In a sense, the mind was the ultimate 'don't get killed' machine: its main job was to look out for anything that might harm you, and help you avoid it.[7] The better our ancestors were at anticipating and avoiding danger, the more they survived and procreated. It follows, then, that the people with the happy minds would have been less able to avoid danger and hence did not live and procreate.

The human mind has evolved over many generations to become highly skilled at detecting and avoiding danger. It is constantly judging and assessing everything we encounter: Is this helpful or harmful? Good or bad? Safe or dangerous? These days we don't have to worry about the sabre-toothed tiger we mentioned in earlier chapters, but instead our mind warns us about performing in our job, being a good parent, paying off debt, getting a disease, caring for elderly parents, or any other of the thousands of things we commonly worry about. In fact, we spend a great amount of time worrying about things that rarely eventuate.

As humans are pack animals, the human mind was also responsible for keeping us as part of a group. Social comparison was developed as a way of keeping us from being rejected from the clan. If you could contribute more to the group, use fewer resources, fit in more than the next person then you would not be the one to be rejected by the group and left to fend for yourself with the tigers.

Similarly, our modern-day minds are continually comparing us against the rest of society (real and imagined) and warning us of rejection.[8] This explains why we worry so much if people like us and we are always looking to improve ourselves in a vain attempt to measure up to an unrealistic measuring stick. But 100,000 years ago we only had a few people in our clan with whom to compare ourselves; now, with modern technology, we have billions. We have created a measuring stick that tells us we are not thin enough, rich enough, smart enough, attractive enough, successful enough, talented enough or good enough in any number of ways. Remember the umbrella of society in Chapter 3. Today all the societal influences, such as the media and electronic communication, foster these comparisons.

For the Stone Age person, more was better. The more weapons you had the more animals you could kill for food. The more food you had the greater the chance of you and your family surviving. The better your cave the safer you and your family were. The more children you had the greater the chance of them surviving to continue your genetic line. In accordance, our modern mind continually looks for more: more power, more love, more status, more success, more money, a bigger house, a fancier car. If we succeed in getting a better paid job, a bigger house and fancier car then we are satisfied – for a moment. But sooner or later we end up wanting more.[9] Again, think about today's umbrella and how the influences encourage us to want more.

Consequently, evolution has shaped our minds so we are predisposed to emotional suffering. We have minds developed to evaluate, compare and criticise ourselves, to be ungrateful for what we have, to focus on what we do not have, and to imagine all types of terrifying scenarios, most of which will never happen. As a result, it is no surprise that we feel anxious and stressed.[10]

So what can we conclude from this information? It appears the good news is that the normal thinking processes of a healthy mind will lead to psychological suffering. Tom isn't defective, and neither are you and I – our minds are doing what they have evolved to do. In fact, it would seem a higher level of psychological suffering may indicate a mind that is doing its job a bit too well!

Feelings and thoughts can be hard to control

As we highlighted earlier in this chapter, the CBT model proposes that the way we think is the way we feel and the way we feel is the way we act. Refer back to Figure 5 showing the model. Then from your experiences with anxiety and stress you would probably know that feelings and thoughts of anxiety and stress are hard to control.

The following exercises have been developed to help you understand some other aspects of this model.

For the first exercise we would like you to hold a pencil in your fingers and think about it for the next five minutes. Describe your experience on the lines below.

_____

_____

_____

_____

How did you go? If you found that your mind was wandering away from the pencil within a few seconds, you are not alone. It is very difficult to focus our thinking, and when we do, we call it concentration. The ability to concentrate varies from person to person but most of us would agree that it is quite difficult to control our thoughts.

The next exercise is taken from a book by Forsyth and Eifert.[11]

PINK ELEPHANT EXERCISE
We would like you to close your eyes and try this: don't think about a pink elephant. Give yourself a few minutes to complete this exercise. Describe your experience on the lines below.

_____

_____

_____

_____

_____

_____

How did you go? Most people find this task impossible because to complete it, you cannot do what the instruction says without thinking of the thing you are not supposed to think about. To explain it another way, the thought 'don't think about a pink elephant' is itself a thought about pink elephants. Consequently, you are caught with the very thing you don't want to do.

Your mind may have tried to devise other clever tactics to accomplish the goal of not thinking about a pink elephant, such as trying to think of something completely different. How was your mind able to do that? How were you able to know that the other thought was not a pink elephant? In order to think of something that is clearly not a pink elephant you need to compare it to a pink elephant. Paradoxically, you are back with the thought of the pink elephant.

Anxiety can be a lot like the pink elephants! The more you think and struggle to get rid of it, the more you are actually thinking about it, and devoting enormous time and energy to trying to control or get rid of the anxiety.

PHRASES EXERCISE
For this exercise we would like you to look at the following phrases that have a word missing. We don't want you to think of the word that is missing. Under no circumstances should you fill in that blank word in your thoughts.

Happily ever _____
Mary had a little _____
If at first you don't succeed, try, try _____
Love conquers _____
Once upon a _____

What was that like? Were you able to control your thoughts and not fill in the missing words? Most people find this task very difficult as these words tend to pop into our head automatically, because these sayings are learnt over a long period of time. This exercise is a good example of how thinking patterns can become so automatic that they pop into our minds without us ever questioning them and sometimes without even being aware of them.

Remember Tom's story? He had many automatic thoughts that he was probably unaware of. Automatic thoughts can be helpful or unhelpful. Tom's mind was hooking him into some unhelpful thinking styles such as 'catastrophising' and 'black and white' thinking. We will explain a range of unhelpful thinking styles below, and as you read through them, see which ones apply to Tom.

Unhelpful thinking styles

Thinking can be helpful at times, and unhelpful at others. Below are some examples of unhelpful thinking styles or patterns.

CATASTROPHISING

This type of thinking focuses on negative possibilities such as pain, loss, rejection, failure or catastrophe. A small mistake may be perceived as a disaster. Self-talk (the messages our judgemental mind sends us) about imminent disasters is usually expressed in thoughts of 'what if . . .' In Tom's example, he was already catastrophising that he would lose his job and his house, after one small mistake with the end-of-month report.

BLACK AND WHITE THINKING

This is the habit of viewing things in an extreme or polarised way, either good or bad, success or failure, positive or negative. There is no middle ground. In reality most situations are neither fantastic nor disastrous but lie somewhere in between. In the example above, when Tom was criticised for his end-of-month report he concluded he was a failure at his whole job and would be fired. By assuming that he has failed his whole company by making one small error, he ignores the fact he is performing above average in other areas of his job.

PERSONALISATION

When we personalise we incorrectly assume that other people's responses are directed at us and we feel responsible for things that are not our fault. For example, Tom felt that if the company lost an important client it would be his fault because his end-of-month report was not as good as his previous reports had been.

JUMPING TO CONCLUSIONS

This thinking error involves drawing negative conclusions without much evidence to support that conclusion. We may assume the worst when things don't unfold as planned and interpret other people's motives and comments in the worst way. Remember in Tom's story, he believed his colleagues were after his job and eagerly waiting for him to get fired. There was not much evidence to support these conclusions.

OVERGENERALISATION

Overgeneralisation involves drawing negative conclusions about ourselves and other people on the basis of little evidence. This thinking error often involves words such as 'always', 'never' and 'everyone'. For example Tom had thoughts like, 'I'll never find a job I like', 'Everyone is talking about my poor performance and is waiting for me to be fired', and 'I always have to perform perfectly to avoid challenges to my management position'.

LABELLING

Labelling is the ultimate overgeneralisation as it ignores the reality that people are an extremely complex mix of behaviours and characteristics, and they cannot be encapsulated by just one or two of these. When we label ourselves or someone else as a loser, failure, idiot or stupid we make gross generalisations over some very specific behaviours. For example, Tom labelled himself an 'anxious person' and a 'failure', based on some very limited behaviours.

BLAMING
Some people tend to blame and condemn other people for their faults. They find it difficult to accept disappointments and human imperfections. The problem with blaming others is that it stops us taking responsibility for ourselves and can prevent us from taking action to change.[12] It can also create bitterness and resentment. In Tom's situation, he blamed his anxiety for him not reaching his true potential in his job.

Dealing with unhelpful thinking

So how do we deal with our thinking when it is unhelpful? Once you are aware of these unhelpful thinking styles and how they are impacting on you in your day-to-day life, you can then begin to let them go or challenge them. Here are some ideas from CBT for dealing with unhelpful thinking.

It is important to recognise that thoughts are not facts – just because we think it, does not mean it is true. Have you ever thought someone was upset with you, but when you checked it out with them, they were not fussed at all? In fact, thoughts are often assumptions.

Check out the evidence for your thought. For example, you might be worried that you might never meet any new friends. Look at what has happened in the past – have you met new people in the past? If you have, it is likely that you will meet new people again.

Sometimes in checking for evidence it is helpful to get feedback from other people. You might be worried that you have said something that will give the wrong impression about you. Asking a friend their thoughts can give a different perspective.

We might need to find an alternative perspective on the situation. Is there another way to view the situation? How would a friend see the situation? What would my therapist say about it? If you were looking at the situation from a distance or from a time in the future, how would you see it?

Ask yourself some questions such as, 'Are my thoughts too black and white?' or 'Am I overgeneralising at the moment?' It might help to look at the exceptions to the situation; for example, a young man might say that he is obsessed about getting a girlfriend and is 'trying too hard all the time'. But when reminded of the times he is pretty relaxed about things and just enjoying doing his own activities, he realises that sometimes he is worrying about it, and sometimes he isn't.

It is also useful to ask yourself whether you are catastrophising the situation. For example, someone might think it would be a disaster if they had a panic episode whilst at a party. But what would that disaster be? The worst that could happen is probably that someone might ask them if they are all right and if they could help. Often we think terrible things are going to happen, but most likely others would not even notice the person was feeling anxious, and if they did, they would probably be kind and helpful.

Change the words in the thoughts – remove 'shoulds', labels and 'what ifs'. Use language that is less harsh and generalising, and use flexible words and phrases, such as 'I would like to' rather than 'I must'.

Reframe or change the thought so that it is less hard on you. You might be thinking, 'I'm such a worrier, I never stop worrying', which could be reframed as: 'I tend to worry, but there are times when I don't and times when I handle my worrying really well.'

Read the two stories below, and think about what strategies Jane's mother and Sam used to deal with the anxious thoughts.

JANE'S STORY

When Jane was about eight years old, she came home from school one day and was very quiet. When her mother, Sue, asked her what was wrong, she said: 'Nobody likes me.' Sue knew this was not true, and the reason she knew this was that Jane was always having friends over to play and going to parties on the weekends.

Sue asked Jane more about the day, and found out that there had been one event that had upset Jane that day. At recess another girl had called Jane an idiot and had run off with some of the other girls, leaving Jane feeling upset.

Sue pointed out that this was one upsetting event in the day, but that she knew Jane was popular with her friends, because she was often invited to play at other kids' places.

Sue also said that calling other children names was not kind, and that Jane was doing well at school and was definitely not an idiot. She asked Jane what she would have thought if a friend had been treated in the same way. Jane said, 'I would have told her it was not fair' and she soon cheered up.

What strategies did Jane's mother use?

_____

_____

_____

_____

_____

Sue checked out the evidence, addressed the 'labelling' that was happening, and found other ways to view the situation.

SAM'S STORY

Sam tended to have times when he would worry, but he had learnt quite a lot about dealing with his thinking. One night a workmate said to him that the boss was saying Sam was not working quickly enough and that Sam often asked questions about things he should know. Sam struggled to know how to handle this feedback. He felt angry that the workmate had said anything to him and that the boss had not said something to him directly, and he felt anxious that maybe it was true.

On the way home he went to a lookout spot over the city. He thought about what had happened, and knew that he was doing a pretty good job. If he asked questions, it was because he needed to, and if he worked slowly, it was because he was working out in his mind how to do the job. He had only been doing the job for a few months, and decided that he was doing a pretty reasonable job. In fact, some people at work had given him compliments on how well he had been doing.

When Sam looked out over the city he saw things in a different way – the thought that came into his mind was that these worries were 'pretty small compared to what was happening in the whole city'. He felt calmer and went home.

What strategies did Sam use?

_____

_____

_____

_____

_____

_____

Sam was able to view the situation from a number of different perspectives, and he also found an exception (the compliments).

Core beliefs

There is another aspect to the CBT model that you may find useful. Have another look at the CBT diagram – imagine there is another arrow feeding into our thoughts. That arrow would come from our 'core beliefs'. These are generalisations about ourselves, others and the world, and they develop as we grow up under the umbrella of society. They tend to be assumptions. Unfortunately some of these core beliefs can be negative and unhelpful; for example, that the world is a dangerous place, 'I'm defective or damaged', or 'I can't cope'. Sometimes we want to be approved of by everyone, competent at all we do and feel always in control.[13,14]

Do any of these ideas ring true for how you view yourself or the world? These beliefs can become traps in your thinking, and trigger stress or anxiety.

If you are having trouble identifying your core beliefs, there are a couple of useful techniques to help you. The first is to identify any themes that arise in your thinking from your increased awareness of your thoughts. These may suggest underlying beliefs about yourself. For example, a theme might be, 'I always mess up and nothing ever goes right for me anyway'.[15] Could you be expecting a lot of yourself or the world?

Another technique is called the 'downward arrow' technique.[16] Take a situation and your thoughts about it, and then ask yourself, 'What does this say or mean about me?' Then repeat this question until you get to the heart of the issue. An example is provided in Figure 6.

FIGURE 6: THE DOWNWARD ARROW TECHNIQUE

I can't seem to keep it together.
(what does this say or mean about me?)

I try hard but then I just lose it.
(what does this say or mean about me?)

I feel out of control.
(what does this say or mean about me?)

I like to be in control.

Note that, depending on the thought, it may be more appropriate to ask, 'What does this say or mean about others . . . or the world?'

So you have identified some unhelpful beliefs; what then? Again, awareness of them may be enough. Or you might like to challenge them and develop more helpful beliefs as you did with thoughts. You might ask yourself, 'How is this belief working for me . . . and how is it working against me?'

Consider one or two of your beliefs and weigh them up in this way.

_____

_____

_____

_____

_____

_____

Mindfulness-based CBT

Mindfulness-based CBT (MBCT) combines the two approaches of CBT and mindfulness, each of which was introduced in Chapter 2 and this chapter. Remember that we said mindfulness refers to paying attention and experiencing the present moment. It is a gentle approach, and when applied to our thinking it means being aware of our thoughts. Sometimes simply being aware is enough to allow you to let the thoughts go.

When you think about it, we actually have a choice whether we run with a particular thought or disengage from it – a bit like going on a train journey, and choosing which train we are going to hop onto. We look at the train number or the destination and make a choice. This is the essence of MBCT and it is very liberating. This awareness also serves to weaken anxious thoughts, and enables you to halt the cycle between anxious thoughts and feelings.[17] The same approach can apply to feelings; for example, when you become aware of anxious feelings early on, you can use your breathing techniques or muscle relaxation to prevent them from escalating.

Taking action

Thoughts and feelings give us useful information and add a great deal to our experience of life. However, sometimes our thoughts and feelings are not accurate and consequently we should not run our lives according to them. For example, you don't have to feel like doing something to do it. How many times have you thought, 'I don't feel like exercising', but you have pushed yourself to exercise and felt much better as a consequence? Similarly, how many times have you thought, 'I don't feel like going to work today', but you got up out of bed and went to work anyway. A large part of our time is taken up performing tasks we don't particularly want to do but we do them because they need to be done. These tasks include washing clothes, preparing meals, doing grocery shopping and cleaning our bodies and houses. We also tend to do these tasks while carrying with us the feelings of boredom or dislike towards these tasks. That is, we don't wait to feel happy before we do what needs to be done.

The idea that we don't have to let strong feelings such as stress and anxiety run our lives has been around for a long time. Morita Therapy was developed by Japanese psychiatrist Shoma Morita, and reflects Eastern views and principles, especially those of Zen Buddhism. The main tenets of Morita Therapy are: accept your feelings; know your purpose; and do what needs to be done. Morita's Zen approach encourages people experiencing anxiety not to focus on their feelings by being more mindful of what they are doing in each moment. By helping people to do what needs to be done, and at the same time paying attention to the quality of that ordinary daily action, this therapy helps people focus less on their thoughts and feelings.[18] This type of mindfulness was described in Chapter 3.

Just remember that one of the easiest ways to deal with troublesome feelings or thoughts is to take action or to change your behaviour. Remember the exercise we asked you to do of standing up and putting your arms out to your sides, and how easy that was to do and control? By taking action we move from a position of little control to a position of total control. The next chapter will focus on taking action, in particular behavioural strategies for managing anxiety.

TRAVEL REMINDERS

Here are some reminders from this chapter. You may want to copy them and make them into a reminder card to place in your diary or wallet, or even on the fridge or a mirror at home.

- **Stress and anxiety can trick and trap us into certain ways of thinking and behaving.**
- **Our thoughts, feelings, and behaviours are intertwined and affect each other.**
- **Unhelpful thinking styles include catastrophising and black and white thinking.**
- **We can learn ways to view a situation differently and be less critical of ourselves.**
- **Sometimes thoughts and feelings are hard to change, so we need to focus on action instead.**

TRAVEL DIARY

AVOIDING AVOIDANCE

Procrastination is the thief of time.

—Edward Young

Although it is pretty close to impossible to fully separate out the cognitive and behavioural aspects of managing stress and anxiety, in this chapter we will focus more on the behaviours associated with stress and anxiety and behavioural treatment strategies which might assist you. These come from an approach known as Behavioural Therapy, which has been around for many years in psychology. We will also consider a couple of useful skills (problem-solving and assertiveness) which may assist you in carrying out these behavioural strategies.

The relationship between fear and avoidance

Anxiety is related to fear. What do we commonly do if we are afraid of something?

Take the example of being afraid of going in a lift: the person who is fearful might climb the stairs instead, even if there are ten floors. This is an avoidant behaviour. Excessive avoidance of anxiety is the issue that is responsible for turning worries, fears and anxieties into life-limiting problems. We can avoid in many different ways, including escape, avoidance, procrastination and safety behaviours.[1] Escape might include the use of drugs and alcohol, safety behaviours might involve superstitious behaviours (such as saying 'touch wood' when we worry that something might not happen) or we might avoid people, places or activities that lead to anxious feelings. However, the basic purpose of avoidant behaviours is to make stress and anxiety disappear. In other words, avoidance is the thread that binds all anxiety problems together.[2]

Let's explain the avoidant behaviours using the stories of the people whom we introduced in Chapter 1, namely Mary, John, Lou and Ashley. Dealing with the sorts of behaviours they display is central to dealing with anxiety. Firstly we will provide some more information and we want you to try to identify which of the avoidant behaviours each person is utilising to deal with the anxiety.

Mary is confident in her work, but becomes very anxious at work social functions. At the Friday night work happy hour, she becomes very anxious and leaves suddenly. Which behaviour/s is Mary using?

_____

_____

John has a fabulous new apartment, but if there is a spider in the apartment, John is out of it. Which behaviour/s is John using?

_____

_____

Lou had a panic attack at the local shopping centre, and now dreads going there. He manages his dread by asking his wife or children to go instead. Which behaviour/s is Lou demonstrating?

_____

_____

Lou also worries about work. He has deadlines and fears that he will not make them. He finds himself spending a lot of time on unimportant jobs and then has to rush near the deadline to get the job done. What is happening here?

_____

_____

Ashley works as a nurse, but worries that she will make a mistake and harm a patient. As a result she constantly checks patient wristbands and notes to make sure she does not make a mistake when giving out medications. What behaviour/s is Ashley using?

_____

_____

If you said that Mary and John used 'escape' behaviours, you would have been correct. These are behaviours that they did right in the midst of the anxiety-provoking situation; that is, they left the situations abruptly. Mary could have used 'avoidance' if she had stayed away from the happy hour altogether, and Lou is definitely avoiding his fear by asking his family to go to the shops for him. Lou is also using 'procrastination'. In other words, he is putting off doing stressful tasks until the last moment. Ashley is using the 'safety' behaviour of checking. Another example of a safety behaviour would be using distraction. Lou might play the card game Patience on the computer all day rather than doing the stressful task, for example.

So why do we use these behaviours? Well, they reduce the fear in the short term. The trouble is that they feed into the sort of vicious cycles we alluded to in Chapter 4. We have anxiety, then we avoid, then the next time we face the same situation we have anxiety and it is very tempting to avoid again. In fact, avoidant behaviours can trap us and the anxiety may become worse. It may also generalise – if you are avoiding the local shops, anxiety may generalise to other shopping centres, so there are more places to avoid. This may be because the individual starts thinking, 'What if I have anxiety (or panic) at that shopping centre too?'

Now honestly answer the following questions:

What do I fear?

_____

_____

_____

_____

How do I escape these fears/avoid them?

_____

_____

_____

_____

Do I procrastinate or use safety behaviours?

_____

_____

_____

_____

_____

We suggest that you talk about these fears with your therapist, and consider trying some of the techniques in the remainder of this chapter, which are all about avoiding avoidance!

Avoiding avoidance!

Have you heard the saying 'If you fall off a horse, the best thing to do is to get straight back on'? This saying suggests that if you avoid an activity you are afraid of, the fear grows bigger, and you might be robbing yourself of the chance to show yourself you can do it. There is a book by Susan Jeffers called *Feel the Fear . . . and Do it Anyway*, which is all about dealing with our fear and anxiety. This book has a great title which also hints at the key behavioural strategy of 'exposure'. This technique came out of early psychology experiments about 'conditioning'. Remember the story of Will who became afraid of bees? Just like Will, we can become conditioned or learn to be afraid of certain triggers or situations. And our brains need to be reconditioned or rewired to not be fearful. The way this is done is through exposure, which involves activating the fear and habituating to it in a controlled way.[3]

In other words, the best way to do 'exposure therapy' is gradually, using the sort of 'baby steps' we mentioned in Chapter 1. Exposure therapy can occur in a number of different ways – for example, a therapist might take the person through a number of role plays. This can be useful in social anxiety or anxiety about social situations. If we think about Mary for a moment again, we will remember that she was fearful of work-related social functions. A helpful strategy for Mary would be to role-play conversations that might arise at one of these functions. A therapist might also talk about useful communication skills that could also help with feeling more confident in such situations. Another example of the use of role play is shown in Meg's story.

MEG'S STORY

Meg was studying occupational therapy. She did very well in her written exams, but was extremely fearful of practical exams. She found that she became very nervous, and noticed that her heart would palpitate and her mouth would become dry. She feared that her mind would go blank and that the examiners would realise she was 'stupid'.

Therapy included role playing the next practical exam. Meg advised her therapist about the topic to be examined, and the sort of questions she might be asked. In the exam she would have to work with a mock patient. In the role play, the therapist became the examiner, and another therapist came in to act as the patient. Meg was asked to explain to the 'patient' things to do with the topic, and then the 'examiner' fired a series of questions. This was role-played about six times, and each time Meg became a bit more comfortable. Meg was also taught breathing and relaxation strategies to assist, and how to challenge some of her self-doubting thoughts. She passed the next exam.

Role playing is useful as it allows the person to rehearse or practise what they would say or do in the feared situation. There is another related technique called 'mental rehearsal' which can also be of assistance. This is when a therapist takes the person gently through the feared situation in a state of relaxation or hypnosis. In doing so the person experiences the situation in a more relaxed state and is conditioned to feel relaxed in the situation. If there is a lot of anxiety, the therapist may begin by guiding the person to watch a movie of themselves in the situation on a screen. Individuals often feel very safe with this technique as they are in an observer role, and they are often less judgemental of themselves in this role.

You can see from Meg's example that these sorts of techniques take effort and time. We will now look at the graded exposure technique, using the example of John, who is fearful of spiders. With graded exposure, we like to make sure that individuals have been taught a number of techniques to help them deal with anxiety symptoms, including breathing and relaxation techniques and some cognitive strategies. We would then ask someone like John a few questions, such as, 'Are there particular types of spiders that you are afraid of? Which colour/size of spiders do you find more frightening? How would you want to get rid of the spider in your apartment?'

Finding out the answers to questions such as these helps determine what factors increase or decrease John's fear. Out of such discussion, the therapist together with John would generate a list of possible scenarios in relation to spiders, and rank them from least anxiety-provoking to most anxiety-provoking. See the left hand column in Table 9 for the list of factors, and the middle column for the ranked degree of anxiety the scenario triggers in John. Remember our rating: 0 = no anxiety and 10 = the most anxiety you have ever experienced. The therapist would then work with John to develop a series of

TABLE 9: JOHN'S GRADED EXPOSURE TABLE

Factors/scenarios	Anxiety 0–10	Graded exposure steps
Small brown spider at a distance	5	1. Looking at pictures of small brown spiders 2. Looking at pictures of small black spiders
Small black spider at a distance	6	3. Looking at pictures of large brown spiders
Large brown spider at a distance	7	4. Looking at pictures of large black spiders
Large black spider at a distance	8	5. Viewing dead spiders in glass containers at the museum from a distance 6. Viewing dead spiders at the museum close up
Small brown spider close up	9	7. Viewing live spiders in glass containers at the museum from a distance
Small black spider close up	10	8. Viewing live spiders in glass containers at the museum close up (less than a minute)
Large brown spider close up	10	9. Viewing live spiders in glass containers at the museum close up (for several minutes)
Large black spider close up	10	10. Holding a jar containing a small dead spider 11. Holding a jar containing a large dead spider 12. Holding a jar containing a small live spider 13. Holding a jar containing a large live spider (less than a minute) 14. Holding a jar containing a large live spider (several minutes) 15. Spraying a spider with insect spray in the apartment or removing

graded exposure steps, and examples of these are shown in the right hand column of the exposure table. John might want to ultimately deal with the spider using insect spray, or he may want to remove the spider from his apartment.

Notice how there are a number of small steps in the graded exposure programme for John, and the least difficult scenario is tackled first, followed by the next difficult and then the next . . . until ultimately John is able to deal with a spider in his apartment. In this way the graded exposure programme is achievable. John will notice that his anxiety will rise when he does each step, but it will then fall. Each step is repeated until it causes less anxiety (at least 50 per cent less) and then John will move on to the next. Sometimes there may be a setback and John will need to return to a previous step and redo that step, then move on to the next one. The programme will take John a good length of time to work through, maybe several months. He will need assistance from the therapist to source the jars with spiders in them. John does not need to be able to have a spider sitting on him; he just needs to be able to deal with one in his apartment.

Tips for dealing with procrastination

Procrastination, or putting things off, is a form of avoidant behaviour. It might be used to avoid a stressful situation, such as a student procrastinating over their assignments and handing them in late as a result. They might even miss an exam as a result of procrastinating. Have a read of Billy's story.

BILLY'S STORY

Billy is studying engineering. He is a capable student, but he has trouble settling down to do his work. Thinking about all the assignments he needs to do makes him feel uncomfortable. He prefers to listen to music, to daydream, to go drinking with his mates . . . anything except study. He is now in trouble as he is very behind with his work. He had supplementary exams to do as well as his usual exams, but he missed them all. He is feeling highly anxious about his future at university.

Do you ever use distractions to avoid doing the jobs you need to do? Sometimes using distractions can serve to help you avoid uncomfortable feelings. Common distractions are going on the Internet, going to the beach, listening to music, watching movies, going out and seeing friends, smoking. Sometimes we are just seeking pleasure in our distractions, which is not a bad thing – but if the cost is too great, then it is a problem.[4]

**Jot down any distractions you experience
on the lines here.**

_____

_____

_____

_____

_____

_____

**Do you make excuses for your procrastination,
such as, 'I'm too busy . . . there's plenty of time and
I'll do it later'? What are some other examples?**

_____

_____

_____

_____

_____

_____

Sometimes there is an element of truth in the excuse, but
sometimes there is little truth, and so one way of dealing with
procrastination is to be honest with yourself.

Another example of procrastination is delaying starting on
your goals, such as exercising. Procrastination can also be
related to expecting too much of yourself and tending to be a
perfectionist. For example, an individual may procrastinate
and be late with a piece of work because they want it to be

perfect. Procrastination may also stem from fear of failure or criticism, a fear of uncertainty, a desire to be approved of by important people in your life or a desire to be in control of things. Sometimes it is related to doubting your abilities.[5]

Do any of these ideas seem to apply to you?
List the relevant ones here.

_____

_____

_____

_____

_____

_____

People who expect a lot of themselves in relation to perfectionism, wanting approval or fear of failure are often quite productive, but having these expectations can cause stress or anxiety and possibly defeat. We need to challenge our thoughts and beliefs in relation to these expectations (have a look back at Chapter 4), and develop new perspectives on ourselves and life.

In terms of wanting to be in control or fear of uncertainty, we need to let go of or challenge some of our ideas as we cannot be in control of everything and life does involve uncertainty. Then we need to challenge our fears by finding ways to get on and do the jobs. We will talk about these strategies more in a moment, and we are going to look into the concept of self-esteem in more detail in Chapter 8.

But first, do you want to make changes in your procrastination behaviours? A powerful way of motivating yourself is to think about how procrastination works for you and how it works against you. Write down your ideas on this here.

_____

_____

_____

_____

_____

How do these ideas keep you procrastinating?
How might they help you behave differently?

_____

_____

_____

_____

_____

Also, if you tend to be a perfectionist, how does this work for you or against you?

_____

_____

_____

_____

_____

What we have been asking you to do is to weigh up the benefits of procrastinating (or being a perfectionist, whichever applies to you) or not procrastinating, and see which comes out in front. We suspect that when you weigh these up, it is likely procrastination or perfectionism works against you more than it does for you.

To deal with perfectionism or procrastination, we can also adopt different behaviours. Remember, the importance of taking action was highlighted at the end of the last chapter. Well, this approach is helpful with procrastination. The way to approach taking action is by setting realistic goals, breaking them down into baby steps, with realistic timeframes. The next step is to get started – even if you don't feel like it, even if there are some uncomfortable feelings associated with the task or even if you would prefer to do something more pleasurable.

In this way you can see that dealing with procrastination involves sitting with your uncomfortable feelings (or exposing yourself to them). There are some strategies that assist with this, including using mindfulness or awareness of the feelings, and to observe these feelings in a non-judgemental way. We will talk more about these strategies in the next chapter on ACT. The principle of surfing the feeling can also be applied here (see page 126).

Remember the saying 'There is no time like the present'? It is very true, so try to focus on the here and now rather than the end result. Be persistent – keep at the task until the job is done, step by step. Remember that effort is the key, and don't forget that it can be good to reward yourself for effort.

What would be good rewards for you (focus on healthy and constructive ones!)?

_____

_____

_____

To illustrate some of these points, now reflect on Zoe's story:

ZOE'S STORY

Zoe has a lot of great ideas about what she could do in life. She thinks enthusiastically about all of them, but then the enthusiasm seems to fade. She has not been able to get started on any of them. Zoe wants to train as a veterinary nurse, and she wants to travel. She has thought about setting up a pet shop with a coffee shop attached, or even volunteering to work in Africa. Zoe remembers that her parents said disapproving things to her when she was growing up, and she had struggled with dyslexia. As a result she thinks of herself as being 'not good enough' as a person.

Zoe told a friend that she was feeling really frustrated about her life, and the friend suggested that they go along to see a life coach together. Zoe needed some convincing but decided she had to do something and went along. The coach talked about how Zoe might think differently about herself and not judge herself. Together they then focused on one of her goals and looked at some small steps to get started on it.

Zoe found the process difficult and it raised some uncomfortable feelings for her. But with support, encouragement, effort and the occasional reward (a massage or going to the movies), Zoe found that the process of working towards her goals became easier as time went on. The coach asked Zoe to keep a diary and to write her goals in it and progress towards them. Together, they kept an eye on her progress. In fact, within twelve months Zoe was working and training as a vet nurse.

What helped Zoe get moving towards one of her goals?

_____

_____

_____

_____

Zoe was helped by the encouragement of her friend and the life coach. The coach helped her to focus on one goal, to keep a diary and give herself some rewards. You can see that setting goals and taking baby steps are a regular theme in this book. We suggest that when setting goals in relation to dealing with procrastination that you think about your priorities. What is the most important task for you to focus on right now, and what can wait? This is different from putting things off that shouldn't be put off. For example, a bill due today takes priority over going shopping. And remember too that often we get a lot of satisfaction and pleasure from achieving our goals and finishing the tasks we need to finish. So good luck with your efforts!

Strategies which may assist on your travels

There are several strategies that may assist you in managing the anxiety, and fit with behavioural approaches.

PROBLEM-SOLVING

Our thoughts and worries can seem overwhelming when we feel stressed or anxious, and so it can be very difficult to think through a problem clearly. Problem-solving, which involves sorting out what the main issues are and looking at practical ways of dealing with them, is a strategy which may assist in working through problems. Problem-solving involves a number of steps and aims to help you settle on the best possible solution for the problem. This may not be a perfect solution, but it will be a start.

Some people like to ask other people their opinion about potential solutions. This can be useful. However, ultimately the individual needs to decide on the best solution as they are the expert on themselves and they are responsible for the consequences of the decision. Remember too that deciding not to make a decision is also a valid option! More time and information may be needed.

With problem-solving, we suggest that you:

- start with more straightforward problems rather than complex ones
- set aside time without distraction to work through the problem (perhaps with the help of your therapist)
- deal with one problem at a time
- make a list of all possible solutions, even if some are a bit wild, as this helps you come up with more ideas.

When planning how to carry out the solution, it is also important to try to be realistic and include plans on how to deal with difficulties that might arise. Remember too that even partial success is a positive outcome.

The steps involved in problem-solving are as follows:

- Define the problem.
- Make a list of all possible solutions.
- Evaluate the solutions; that is, think about the advantages and disadvantages of each solution.
- Choose the best possible solution.
- Plan how to carry it out – this involves breaking the solution down into small steps.
- Review your progress. [6,7,8]

To illustrate problem-solving, consider the story of Jade.

JADE'S STORY

Jade was unhappy in her work as a personal assistant. Her boss did not know how to communicate what he wanted done, and when jobs weren't completed as he wanted, he got angry. Jade had always wanted to study art and design, but did not feel confident enough to pursue this avenue. Her parents had always told her to get a job and save up for a house – 'Art won't pay the bills'. Jade felt down and worried about her future as she did not want to be in a job forever that she really didn't like. She did not know what to do to turn things around.

The process of problem-solving would assist Jade to work through this dilemma. We have completed the steps for Jade in the next section, and also left extra space for you to try this strategy with a problem of your own.

Step 1: Define the problem

JADE: 'I'm unhappy in my work and my boss doesn't communicate with me. I am worried about my future in this sort of job. I don't find it satisfying, and have always wanted to get involved in something artistic, but I don't have the confidence to make a change.'

Lines for you:

_____

_____

_____

_____

Step 2: Make a list of all possible solutions

JADE:

- Quit my job and study art and design full-time.
- Go part-time in my current job and study part-time.
- Find a new part-time job, such as in an art shop or café, and study art part-time.
- Show someone who works in art and design my art and get some feedback to build my confidence.
- Try to sort out the problems with my boss.
- Win the lottery and just paint!

Lines for you:

_____

_____

_____

_____

Step 3: Weigh up the advantages and disadvantages of each possible solution

JADE:

- Advantages and disadvantages of 'quit my job and study art and design full-time' – I would love to just be doing art and design, and to be out of my job, but this is pretty risky. I need money to live.
- Advantages and disadvantages of 'go part-time in my current job and study part-time' – this could work, if my boss would let me. I guess I don't know until I ask, and at least I would be doing some art and earning some money at the same time. Studying part-time would take longer, but that's okay.
- Advantages and disadvantages of 'find a new part-time job, such as in an art shop or café, and study art part-time' – I would love to have a job change, and can see myself working in a café or art shop. It would depend on whether I could find a job, and the part-time study seems sensible.
- Advantages and disadvantages of 'show someone who works in art and design my art and get some feedback to build my confidence' – this sounds scary, but may be possible if I found someone I felt a bit comfortable with.
- Advantages and disadvantages of 'sort out the problems with my boss' – well, I would need to do this if I ended up staying there, but otherwise I might as well leave it, it's hard to talk with him.
- Advantages and disadvantages of 'win the lottery and just paint!' – this sounds great, but is not so realistic.

Lines for you:

_____

_____

_____

_____

_____

_____

Step 4: Out of your options, choose the best possible solution

JADE: 'I think going part-time and studying part-time is the answer. I could ask my boss if I can go part-time, but I like the idea of finding a different part-time job. I might check that out first.'

Lines for you:

_____

_____

_____

_____

_____

_____

_____

Step 5: Planning – in small steps

JADE:

- Look into art and design courses
- See what I can do part-time
- Look on the Internet first
- Then phone with any queries
- See if I can find a job in a café or art shop
- Get my résumé up to date
- Check for jobs on-line
- Drop résumé in to a number of places
- If there are no other jobs, speak with boss about going part-time
- Once work is sorted out, enrol in art course.

Lines for you:

_____

_____

_____

_____

_____

_____

_____

_____

Step 6: Review how the problem-solving is going after a couple of weeks

JADE: After two weeks, Jade has found a course that she wants to do and is working on getting her résumé up-to-date.

Lines for you:

_____

_____

_____

_____

_____

_____

_____

ASSERTIVENESS

As we mentioned earlier, it can be useful to develop communication skills to improve confidence and allay anxiety in different situations. One useful communication skill is assertiveness. Consider Jade's situation again: for Jade to communicate with her boss about difficult issues, assertiveness, or being able to express her needs more directly, would be helpful. So what does assertiveness involve and how can we develop it?

Assertiveness involves changing the ways in which you relate to people and the behaviours that you use, and it can be helpful in responding to criticism, saying 'no' to requests or starting conversations with people in social situations. It is based on the fact that you as an individual have some rights, including respecting yourself (as well as others) and meeting your needs. Other rights include changing your mind, needing time to think things over before making a decision and asking for what you want. Also, you are not responsible for the behaviour of other adults.

There are three different types of behaviours, namely passive, assertive and aggressive behaviours. Passive behaviour is the opposite of assertive behaviour, and it involves avoiding saying what you think or feel, and putting other people's needs above your own. Does this sound familiar? With aggressive behaviour, we show our frustration and tend to offend others, perhaps by talking over them or showing aggression in some other behaviour. Assertive behaviour on the other hand involves communicating thoughts and feelings clearly and letting people know, in a respectful way, when something does matter to you.[9,10,11]

We learn assertive and non-assertive behaviours as we grow up. Remember the umbrella of society which influences us? Our family, friends and school, for example, teach us how to behave. How did your family members deal with conflict – did they ignore it, or become aggressive? What did they do when they disagreed with someone – did they assert their rights or keep quiet?

Consider what you learnt about being passive, assertive or aggressive as you grew up and since then, and jot down your ideas.

_____

_____

_____

_____

_____

_____

_____

What about your behaviour would you like to be different now?

_____

_____

_____

_____

_____

_____

So, how can we learn to be more assertive? We have found in our practice that it is helpful to learn to use 'I' statements. If Jade was going to use such a statement to talk to her boss it would sound like this: 'I can see that you are feeling annoyed about this job. However, I feel upset when you say that I "haven't done the job as you would like" because you did not give me any instructions. When you pick on my work it affects my confidence. I would prefer that you said clearly what you wanted, so that I can follow your instructions.'

Look at what is involved in Jade's statement. She talked about:

- her feelings about her boss's behaviour and the effect of the behaviour ('I feel . . .')
- what the unacceptable behaviour was in a non-blameful way ('when you . . .')
- the effects of the behaviour on herself ('because . . .')
- what she wants to happen ('I would prefer . . .')[12]
- Jade also acknowledged her boss at the start, when she said 'I can see that you feel . . .'

When speaking assertively, it is important to stand or sit in an upright position and not to fidget. We suggest that you have an open body posture (no folded arms or crossed legs), speak in a clear and calm tone of voice and use eye contact. The key is to practise – with your therapist, or a friend or even in the mirror. You might consider writing down what you want to say before you practise. If the person does not respond as you wish, you might need to repeat your statement, or suggest that you talk about it again at another time.

TRAVEL REMINDERS

Here are some reminders from this chapter. You may want to copy them and make them into a reminder card to place in your diary or wallet, or even on the fridge or a mirror at home.

- **Anxiety is related to fear, and we often avoid situations associated with fear.**
- **Other avoidance behaviours include escape, procrastination and safety behaviours.**
- **One treatment for anxiety (and avoidance) is gradual exposure, in a step-by-step way.**
- **Sometimes we procrastinate (especially if we are perfectionists) to manage anxiety, but this leads to its own problems. Setting goals, getting started and sitting with the feelings can help.**
- **Other strategies that might help with anxiety are problem-solving and learning to be more assertive.**

TRAVEL DIARY

STRUGGLE LESS AND SIT WITH YOUR FEELINGS

*Water is fluid, soft and yielding.
But water will wear away the rock,
which is rigid and cannot yield. As
a rule, whatever is fluid, soft and
yielding will overcome whatever is
rigid and hard.*

—Lao Tzu (4th–6th century BC)

This chapter continues the focus of the last chapter, namely behavioural strategies for stress and anxiety, and in particular it will focus on effort and action which are central to change. Words are just words if behaviour is not changed. For example, if your partner comes home later than expected and says sorry for being late chances are you will accept his/her apology. However, if this behaviour continues to happen you may begin to question how much they really mean it when they say that they are sorry. Without an effort to change the offending behaviour, sorry is just a word that quickly loses its meaning. The same can be said of the phrase 'I love you'. If someone is telling their partner 'I love you', but they don't help with any household chores, or consider their partner in any of their decisions and they hardly spend time with their partner, then these words can become meaningless.

Several of the psychological approaches incorporated into this book focus on purpose, action and acceptance, including Constructive Living, and Acceptance and Commitment Therapy (ACT). As we mentioned at the end of Chapter 4, the idea that we don't have to let strong feelings such as stress and anxiety run our lives has been around for a long time. We spoke of Morita Therapy, which advocates acceptance of your feelings, knowing your purpose and doing what needs to be done. Morita encourages individuals experiencing anxiety not to focus on their feelings by being more mindful.[1]

ACT receives its name from one of its central principles, namely taking action. This relates to accepting what is out of our control, and taking action that helps create a rich and meaningful life.[2] It is important to recognise that thinking and feeling 'well' does not necessarily mean that you will live a rich and meaningful life, and thinking and feeling 'poorly' does not mean you can't live a rich and meaningful life. ACT proposes that struggling with anxiety-provoking thoughts and feelings is the problem, and the solution is for people to learn how to develop comfort in their own bodies and minds while still having these anxious thoughts and feelings.[3]

In short, ACT advises us to stop the struggle to think and feel better! It suggests that instead you focus on what you can control or what you can do to live a meaningful life. The idea is to become less caught up in the pain in our bodies and heads, and get more involved in doing what we care about and value. This involves changing your relationship with stress and anxiety, as most of us spend our time trying to reduce painful thoughts and feelings. This is a struggle that may result in increased uncomfortable bodily feelings (by stimulating the sympathetic nervous system). It is also hard work and can be exhausting and may make your memory worse because your attention is diverted to the anxiety. It will give you short-term relief but does not work in the long term, and it stops you actively engaging in your own life.[4]

Let's now explore the ACT model in more detail, and look at some of the strategies for anxiety specifically from ACT. This is an opportunity for you to explore some different ideas and see how they fit for you as an individual.

The ACT model

The ACT model incorporates six central processes that are part of a whole:

- contact with the present moment
- defusion
- acceptance
- self-as-context
- values
- committed action.

We will explain each of these processes in a moment. The ACT model presents these processes as the six points on a hexagon, as shown in Figure 7 overleaf.

ACT proposes that these processes enable us to develop greater 'psychological flexibility', which is defined as being able to be in the present, aware and open to our experience, and to take action consistent with our values.[5] The ACT acronym summarises the approach:

A = Accept your thoughts and feelings, and be present.
C = Choose a valued direction.
T = Take action.

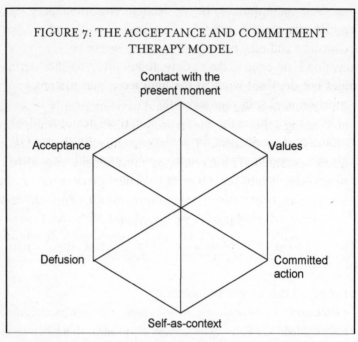

FIGURE 7: THE ACCEPTANCE AND COMMITMENT
THERAPY MODEL

Contact with the
present moment

Acceptance

Values

Defusion

Committed
action

Self-as-context

Source: Adapted from Harris, R. 2009, *ACT Made Simple: An easy-to-read primer on Acceptance and Commitment therapy*, New Harbinger Publications, United States of America.

ACT also talks about human language and its complexities. It sees the mind as being reliant on language and all the symbols of language (such as naming, comparing, planning or remembering). ACT views the mind as working for us in some ways and against us in others. It enables us to create, learn and communicate, but it can be used to lie or deceive, to dwell on past painful events, scare ourselves or create unhelpful stories about ourselves.[6] The next chapter will also highlight language and stories in the context of Narrative Therapy.

When incorporated into therapy, the ACT model and these principles are explained by the therapist, and the individual is taken through strategies based on them. We will now describe each of the principles and then share some of the ACT strategies which are useful in anxiety.

CONTACT WITH THE PRESENT MOMENT

This refers to being physically and psychologically present, and paying attention to the moment, rather than drifting into our automatic thoughts.[7] This process stems from Buddhist traditions and is consistent with mindfulness and MBCT principles. Consider also the earlier discussion about neuroplasticity of the brain in relation to the use of mindfulness in therapy. Mindfulness is an integral part of the ACT model and assists the individual to develop psychological flexibility and achieve lasting change in behaviours.

DEFUSION

Defusion is the opposite of 'fusion', which means being joined or attached. We can become 'fused' or very attached to our thoughts. The thought can seem to be the absolute truth, a thought that must be obeyed, or something you won't let go of even if it hinders you. In the context of ACT, defusion means separating or stepping back from our thoughts, images and memories, and holding them gently rather than tightly. The metaphors of watching our thoughts as if they were clouds floating across the sky, or a car, bus or train going past, are often used.

In ACT, individuals are asked to notice their thoughts. The therapist uses questions such as, 'Can you notice what your thoughts are now?' or 'What is your mind telling you now?' The individual is also asked about whether the thought is helpful, or if the thought is followed, 'Will it take you in the direction of a rich (and) meaningful life, or will it keep you stuck?'[8]

ACCEPTANCE

Acceptance in the context of ACT refers to making room for our feelings, even the painful ones (such as anxiety), and reducing the struggle with them. It does not mean liking them, but is about sitting with them for a while.[9] This process stems from the philosophy of ACT and also the behavioural approach of exposure which was highlighted in Chapter 5, and ACT provides strategies for working on acceptance. We will also explore the concept of acceptance further in Chapter 9.

SELF-AS-CONTEXT

This process relates to the mind, and the concept that there are two separate parts to the human mind or human consciousness: that is, our 'thinking self' or thinking mind and our 'observing self'. We can easily know the thinking self, as we have a constant stream of thoughts. The observing self is the part of us from which we observe feelings, thoughts, sensations, memories, urges, sights, sounds, smells, tastes and memories. This is the part of us that is able to 'step back' and observe these things and remain separate from them. This part of us does not get hooked up in what our judgemental mind is telling us. You know that you are thinking because this part of you called the observing self is able to observe your thoughts. This is the same for your feelings and actions – you know you are feeling and doing because part of you is observing these things. The observing self enables our capacity for self-awareness.[10]

The observing self has many special qualities including being the source of true acceptance. It observes everything you do and never judges you, and it cannot be improved upon in any way. The observing self has been there with you from birth to death and is unchanging. It is always there, whether we forget about it or don't even know about it. In hypnotherapy training, we learnt about 'the hidden observer' of our mind.[11]

This is a part of the mind which looks after us when we are relaxing or asleep, for example, and is utilised in many hypnotherapy techniques.

To further explain the thinking and observing parts of the mind, consider a provocative teen. The thinking mind, just like the teen, is not governed by rules such as facts, sense, helpfulness or compassion. Rather, it is governed by the rules of getting a reaction at all costs. If you have ever argued with a teenager you will understand how skilled they are at hooking you into an argument and pushing for any signs of a reaction such as a raised voice or annoyed facial expression. If the teen gets a whiff of a reaction they go in harder, and the rules of engagement for the teen seem to be relentless. They never give up, and will follow you from room to room if they have hooked you into justifying or answering back. However, if you let their words wash over you and let them be, and don't argue with them, they soon stop talking and go away. The thinking mind is similar to this. No amount of reasoning, justifying or pleading will stop it sending the thoughts your way. The best strategy may be to engage the observing part of the mind to just let the thoughts be, accept that they are there and not be hooked by them.

VALUES

We introduced the concept of values in Chapter 2, when we asked you to consider the different domains in life such as relationships or work, and what was important to you in each area. Being clear about values is central to creating a rich and meaningful life.[12] Most of our time is spent doing things we don't feel like doing, such as washing, cleaning or paying bills. We do them because they need to be done. So why do we go to work even if we don't feel like it? Many would say just for the money, but many would say for other values, such as they believe their work is important or meaningful, or they appreciate being able to provide for their family, which is very important to them. Values are central and it is important to regularly remind ourselves to come back to our values, especially when we feel lost or overwhelmed.

COMMITTED ACTION
This relates to taking action which is guided by our values. Harris says that it means 'doing what it takes', even if it brings up some discomfort. Making an appointment with a therapist and arriving at the appointment, reading this book and doing the exercises, or doing some regular relaxation are examples of committed action. You can take committed action by choosing a domain in life that you want to work on, focusing on what you value in this domain and setting some goals, as we asked you to do in Chapter 2.[13] Also, any of the behavioural strategies described in Chapter 5, and which avoid avoidance, fit with the process of committed action and can be incorporated into ACT.

ACT strategies

In this section we will describe some of the ACT strategies which are designed to address one or more of the above processes. You may want to just read about the strategies, or you may feel confident enough to try them with your therapist, or on your own if you feel able to. You may want to try one or two at a time, and return to this section when you are ready to try another one or two. With each strategy, consider which of the above processes (contact with the present moment, defusion, acceptance, self-as-context, values, committed action) are involved. There will be space to write down your ideas at the end of each exercise.

IMAGINE THIS
This exercise is based on examples provided by Russ Harris.[14]

THOUGHT-NOTICING EXERCISE

Make yourself comfortable and close your eyes. Imagine a recent experience which triggered some worrying thoughts (choose an uncomfortable, but not distressing, experience). Notice the thoughts. Identify one of them and add the prefix, 'I am having the thought that . . . '

Then identify another thought, but this time say the thought in the voice of a cartoon or television character. Notice your response when you do this.

Now think about the worrying situation again and identify another thought. This time try singing the thought to a tune that you know well, such as 'Happy birthday'.

When you have finished exploring these ideas, focus on the sounds that you can hear around you, open your eyes and come back to the room.

What happened when you said, 'I'm having the thought that . . .' or said the thought in a different voice, or sang the thought?

_____

_____

_____

_____

_____

_____

What ACT process does this exercise demonstrate?

_____

_____

_____

_____

In our experience, using these strategies lessens the worry associated with these thoughts. The thoughts may even seem to be humorous! In this way, this exercise demonstrates the process of defusion.

LEAVES ON A STREAM
This exercise is adapted from Forsyth and Eifert.[15]

LEAVES AND THOUGHTS EXERCISE
Make yourself comfortable and let your eyes close. Imagine that you are sitting beside a gentle stream, and there are leaves flowing past on the surface of the water. Over the next few minutes, observe each thought that comes into your mind. Then take a thought and imagine placing it on a leaf, and let it float by. If a feeling pops up, observe the feeling and say, 'Here's a feeling of . . . ' and place it on a leaf. When you are ready, gently open your eyes and come back to the room.

How did you find this exercise?

_____

_____

_____

What ACT processes were involved in the exercise?

_____

_____

_____

_____

This technique is also related to the process of defusion. There are similar techniques in Hypnotherapy, such as gathering up some leaves or twigs and attaching to each one a feeling or thought, then placing them on a stream and letting them float downstream. Or placing boxes which represent feelings or thoughts into the basket below a hot air balloon, and letting them float far away.

UNPACKING THE ACCEPTANCE OF EMOTIONS

The following exercise is adapted from Russ Harris.[16]

BEING WITH AN EMOTION EXERCISE

Identify the feeling you want to work with, such as anxiety. Notice the feeling and where you feel it in the body. You might feel it in the chest or stomach. What shape or colour does it look like? Then imagine gently breathing into it, and keep breathing in and out to that spot in the body. Then allow some space around the feeling and sit with it for a while. Just allow it to be there, and breathe. Sit with it for a while, breathe into it, and notice what happens with the feeling. When you are ready, open your eyes and come back to the room.

How did you find this exercise?

_____

_____

_____

_____

_____

What ACT processes were involved in the exercise?

_____

_____

_____

_____

_____

Generally an emotion is felt intensely at the start, but it fades quite quickly. This technique is related to the process of acceptance and defusion. It illustrates sitting with an emotion and allowing the feelings. We will talk more about acceptance in Chapter 8.

The next few strategies are drawn from the work of Forsyth and Eifert.[17] Again, consider whether you want to work on these by yourself or with your therapist, or whether it is best to leave them for a while.

TRY, TRY AS HARD AS YOU CAN

For this exercise, we would like you to again focus on the pencil you used in the concentration exercise in Chapter 4.

TRYING EXERCISE

We would like you to try to pick up the pencil. Try really hard to pick up that pencil. If you find yourself actually picking up that pencil, stop. That was not the instruction, the instruction was to try to pick up the pencil.

Describe your experience on the lines below.

_____

_____

_____

_____

_____

_____

How did you go? If you found that after some effort your mind was saying, 'I can't follow that instruction – either I pick the pencil up or I don't', then you're exactly right. There is no way to try to pick up the pencil and at the same time actually pick it up. Trying is a form of 'not doing'.

Many people get caught in the trap of trying. It is much more helpful to be really aware of your level of willingness to do something. If your willingness is complete, then go ahead and do it, and if your willingness is not complete, then don't do it. Willingness only has an on/off switch; either you are or you are not. You cannot be a bit willing, just like a woman can't be a bit pregnant.[18]

Which ACT processes were involved in the exercise?

_____

_____

_____

_____

_____

_____

In a different way, this exercise also illustrates defusion. It also involves awareness and action.

ROOM FOR THOUGHT

We would like you to get into your relaxation position for this exercise and begin with some diaphragmatic breathing as you learnt in Chapter 3. Keep this slow, deep and steady breathing going for the entire exercise.

THOUGHTS AND ROOMS EXERCISE

Imagine your mind is a white room with two doors at either end of the room. Thoughts come IN through one door and leave OUT the other door. Watch each thought as it enters the IN door. As you pay attention to the thought, label it as either a judging thought or a non-judgemental thought.

Observe the thought as it makes its way across the room to the OUT door and leaves. Don't judge the judgement, don't analyse it or hold on to it. Don't believe or disbelieve it; just notice the thought and acknowledge it. It's just a moment in time, a brief visitor in the white room that is your mind. It is nearly impossible to stop your mind

coming up with these judgements. Your mind will constantly evaluate and judge your experiences. Notice if you are judging yourself for having the thought. Don't try to change the judgement, justify it or argue with it. Just acknowledge it for what it is and label it: there is 'judging', there is 'worry'.

Recognising judgemental thoughts and not getting trapped or hooked in by them is the goal of this exercise. The length of time each thought stays in the room and the intensity of your emotional reaction will guide you as to whether you are getting hooked by certain thoughts. Continue noticing, continue the deep breathing and continue labelling. A thought is just a thought; it is not a fact or the truth. It is not the truth about you; it does not totalise you as a person and it is not the boss of you. Each thought does not mean you have to react. Observe your thoughts as if they were visitors passing in and out of the white room. Let them have their brief moment of your attention, they are fine the way they are. Let the judging thoughts and all the other uninvited visitors just be; let them enter the room and leave the room without reaction, without struggle. Then you are ready to greet and label the next thought . . . and the next.

Keep doing this exercise until you feel a real emotional shift and a growing distance from your thoughts. Continue doing the exercise until the judgements are no longer bossing, no longer demanding action and no longer important. Wait until the thoughts and judgements are fleeting and take but a moment for you to watch them come in and out of the room. When you are ready you can gently open your eyes and come back to the here and now.

Practise this exercise at least once a day. As with any other skill, learning to be an observer of automatic thoughts and feelings takes practice. This is another way to practise mindfulness, just staying in the moment and paying attention to your experience just how it is. Recognising how the mind tries to trick and trap you is a useful skill. It can be an important step away from the old relationship with avoidance and struggle and towards learning to relate to your mind in a different way.[19]

Which ACT processes were involved in this exercise?

_____

_____

_____

_____

_____

This exercise introduces the idea of observing and accepting our thoughts, and not being hooked into judgements about your experience. It also involves being in the present moment.

OH, WHAT A _____ LILY
Again, get into your relaxation position and take a few deep and relaxing breaths before you begin.

LILY EXERCISE
Now gently close your eyes and imagine a lily that has just been freshly cut from a garden after a summer shower of

rain. Take time to notice the lily fully, using as many of your senses as possible. Focus your eyes on the colour, patterns and shape of the lily. Notice the light and shadows that the rain droplets make on the petals. Notice the intricate patterns of decoration on each petal. Move the lily to your nose so you can smell its perfume. Touch the petals and stem with your fingertips to fully appreciate the textures and contours of this flower. Listen to the petals, stem and leaves as you explore them; do they make any sound? Pay attention fully to the qualities of the freshly cut lily and your experience of it.

As you were completing this exercise your mind may have provided evaluations of the lily. Your mind could have suggested, 'What a beautiful lily' or 'This lily smells lovely'. Your mind may have provided some negative evaluations too such as, 'This lily stinks; it's giving me a headache' or 'I hate lilies, and this one is really ugly'. Your mind may have even accessed certain memories of receiving a loving gift of flowers or perhaps a frightening hospital stay.

The point to this exercise is to get you to realise that your evaluations of the lily don't change the lily one bit. The lily is a lily regardless of what your mind calls it. Similarly, your evaluations of the lily are not the lily. The lily will not change just because your mind labels it this or that.[20]

It is nearly impossible to stop your mind coming up with these judgements. Your mind will constantly evaluate and judge your experiences. This is an exercise for helping you see reality as it is, not as your judgemental mind and past history says it is. Mindful acceptance is an extremely useful tool to help you recognise when you are hooked up in evaluations of your experience, rather than the raw experience itself. For example, when you are feeling anxious, instead of getting caught up in evaluations of those feelings like 'this is terrible, I can't handle this, I have to get out of here', it may be more useful to accept, acknowledge and notice the raw experience for what it is. For example: 'My heart is racing, my hands are sweaty, my breathing is fast. I don't like these feelings but I can accept them and not run away.'

Acceptance often involves doing something counterintuitive. It means learning to stay with your experience and leaning into the racing heart, sweaty hands and fast breathing when every sinew in your body is telling you to pull away. Acceptance means acknowledging and making room for the discomfort, allowing it to be, without doing anything about it and without trying to make it go away. When you are observing your thoughts there is no good or bad, right or wrong – there is just noticing, experiencing and learning. Acceptance will allow you to think your thoughts as they are and not as your mind tells you they are. This will create space for you to feel your emotions and not struggle with them or run away from them.

Which ACT processes were involved in this exercise?

_____

_____

_____

_____

_____

_____

This exercise involves being in the present moment and acceptance.

WHAT'S IN A NAME?

This exercise can be done anytime and anywhere worries and anxious thoughts appear. It is designed to give you skills to go against some urges that may have been pushing you around. Instead of moving back from your discomfort you are leaning into it. Instead of stiffening with your discomfort you are softening to it and you are starting to uncover the tricks and traps of your critical and judgemental mind. This exercise can be useful when you are trying to resist anxious thoughts and urges.

LABELLING EXERCISE

For this exercise, you will require some index cards or pieces of paper. When any worries and anxiety show up, simply label them, placing each thought, worry, sensation, urge or image on its own card. For example, 'I'm not good enough', 'I can't do this', 'I can't breathe', 'My heart is pounding', 'I have to get out of here', 'I'm a failure', 'Everyone is looking at me', 'I can't cope' or 'People think I am an idiot'.

Before writing on the cards, the urges and thoughts were in your head, where they can grow and became big and powerful in the dark. They were heavy, hard and bossy in there. Now that they have been put out into the light, written on a card and exposed, you can see them easily. They seem to already be shrinking in size and power now that you can see them for what they are: just thoughts, urges, sensations, images. They are not the truth. Now you are able to choose to be bossed by what is on the card, or you can allow what you wrote to just be. Just as it is . . . an urge . . . a thought . . . an image . . . a sensation.

There is no need to struggle anymore. In the past you have fought with the things on the cards. To understand that fight, place the card with the sensation, thoughts or urge on it between your hands (with hands held flat) and push your hands together as hard as you can for 30 seconds. Now place the card gently on your lap. Take a moment to reflect upon the difference in energy needed between pushing against the thought or urge compared to the sensation of the card simply laying on your lap.

Now that you have uncovered these thoughts and urges and revealed them for what they are, you can practise travelling and taking those urges and thoughts along for the ride without them determining the direction of your journey. Simply put the cards in your bag or pocket as you carry out your daily activities. You can keep travelling in the direction of your values with these cards going along with you. You don't have to get rid of the cards before doing what you want to do. You can take them out and look at them and choose whether you are going to be hooked by their tricks and traps or not. The choice is yours. [21]

Which ACT processes were involved in this exercise?

_____

_____

_____

_____

_____

This exercise involves defusion, acceptance, self-as-context and committed action.

Did you find these exercises helpful? What ideas can you hold onto from them to help you in your day-to-day life?

_____

_____

_____

_____

_____

_____

Travel is never easy

Travel is often an exciting experience, but it always has challenges. Sometimes sorting out travel plans and timetables can be tricky, or dealing with foreign languages or currency, inclement weather or loneliness. The concept of life not being easy is not new, as philosophers have alluded to for many years. More recently, former Australian Prime Minister Malcolm Fraser said: 'Life was not meant to be easy.' This statement was based on his belief in self-discipline and individual sacrifice in the cause of national progress.[22]

So, the idea of life being a challenge at times is an old one, but it is funny how many of us are still searching for the easy way. When people come to therapy and ask how they can overcome their stress or anxiety, they may really be asking 'Is there an easy way?' You have probably already learnt that success and happiness rarely come easily and rarely come at all for those who give up, do nothing or wait. Any change requires courage, effort and willingness. Things won't change until we find the willingness, despite the fear and anxiety that we may feel, to do what fits with what we value in life.

JULIE'S STORY

Julie had struggled with anxiety for many years. One way the anxiety showed itself was with urges to eat a lot of food. Julie could identify that she looked to food for comfort when she was bored, stressed or anxious. She would feel the anxious feelings in her shoulders and her chest, and these seemed to be relieved for a short while by eating. Then the feelings of guilt and shame would take over. She felt desperate to change this pattern of eating as it was impacting on her health and her relationships.

Julie had tried everything, from diets to therapists to distraction, but nothing seemed to help. It was explained to Julie that she could notice her feelings and thoughts around the time she had the urge to eat. She had tried to avoid them in the past, and it took courage to stop avoiding them. But now she had a way to notice them and to sit with them. She had a strategy to manage them, by breathing in and out to them and to make space for them. Julie was 'blown away' by this idea. She had to make the effort to use the strategy, but she was amazed at how it helped her.

Approaches such as ACT and Constructive Living incorporate the philosophy that few things that are worthwhile in life are easy, that living well and in accordance with your values can be plain hard work, and that pain and suffering are also part of living well. When you open up your life you also open up to pain, in its various forms. It seems funny to think that in order to 'have it all', you really need to have it all – the good, the bad and the pain as well. Sometimes to get the life we want we can't take the easy way, we need to open up to difficulty. Therefore with effort, courage and willingness we can achieve what is important to us, as reflected in this quote from George Bernard Shaw in Back to Methuselah: 'Life was not meant to be easy, my child, but take courage: it can be delightful.'[23]

TRAVEL REMINDERS

Here are some reminders from this chapter. You may want to copy them and make them into a reminder card to place in your diary or wallet, or even on the fridge or a mirror at home.

- **ACT focuses on accepting what is out of our control and taking action that helps to create a rich and meaningful life.**
- **It incorporates six central processes, including contact with the present moment, defusion, acceptance, self-as-context, values and committed action.**
- **ACT suggests that these enable us to develop greater psychological flexibility.**
- **There is a range of practical strategies which help us develop these processes.**
- **Life has challenges, and change requires courage and effort.**

TRAVEL DIARY

STORIES THAT HELP

*A good traveller has no fixed plans
and is not intent on arriving.*

—Lao Tzu (4th–6th century BC)

One of the therapies we introduced in Chapter 2 was Narrative Therapy, which focuses on helping an individual define what they want in life and how best to use their own knowledge and skills to achieve that. We believe this is a useful and respectful approach.

There are a number of central ideas in Narrative Therapy, such as stories, making meaning, the effect of 'dominant' stories and our social context. We will explore each of these ideas in this chapter and consider how narrative approaches might help in the management of stress and anxiety.

All about stories

Stories are essential to understanding Narrative Therapy ideas. Conversations using Narrative Therapy are sometimes referred to as 're-authoring or re-storying' conversations. In the context of Narrative Therapy, stories are made up of: events, linked in sequence, across time and according to a plot. We create stories about our lives to help ourselves make the daily events of our lives meaningful. We link particular events together in a certain order across a time period in a way that makes sense to us.

We all have lots of stories about our lives, happening at the same time. For example, we have stories about ourselves, our abilities, our struggles, our dreams, our achievements, our failures, our work and our relationships, to name a few. The way we have developed these stories is determined by how we have linked certain events together in a sequence and by the meaning we have given to them. This meaning forms the plot of the story. We are constantly giving meanings to our experiences, as we live our lives.[1]

ROSE'S STORY

Rose has a story about herself 'panicking over nothing'. She has strung together a number of events that have happened to her which involve 'overreacting and becoming very anxious' in situations that other people seem to deal with easily. As a demonstration of her 'panicking over nothing' she has selected out many events. These events include: getting upset when her four-year-old daughter falls over, failing her driving test and losing the singles tennis finals. These events have been selected out and privileged over other events, as they fit with Rose's plot of 'panicking over nothing'.

As each new event is chosen and incorporated into the dominant story (plot), Rose's story gains richness and thickness. As it gains thickness, other events of Rose's anxiety and tendency to get easily stressed are more readily remembered and added to the story. During this

---

process, the story thickens and becomes even richer and more dominant in Rose's life. In addition, it becomes easier and easier for Rose to find more and more events that are congruent with the meaning she has reached.

These events of 'panicking over nothing' that Rose is recollecting are privileged over other events that do not fit with the dominant plot of 'panicking over nothing'. For example, the time Rose got bitten by a friend's dog and was very calm, the time she helped an injured child, and when she passed her driving test. These events are not being elevated in their significance and may be seen as a fluke, given that the dominant plot of Rose's story is about 'panicking over nothing'. When stories are retold there are many events that are not selected because they do not fit with the dominant plot.

Rose's family have also contributed to her being able to believe she is 'panicking over nothing'. They have selected out stories of Rose's 'anxiousness' right back to the day she was born. Rose's family and friends have always made a significant contribution to her view of herself as being 'anxious' by frequently reflecting on this quality when talking about Rose.[2]

We live lots of stories at the same time

Different stories can be told about the same events and lots of stories can be happening at the same time. No single story can completely cover all the contingencies of life or be free of contradiction or ambiguity. For example, if Rose attended sessions with a narrative therapist, an alternative story about her ability to function under pressure may develop. Other events, Rose's interpretations of those events and other people's interpretations of those events may lead to Rose developing an alternative story about her abilities in tricky situations, a story of Rose being 'calm under pressure'.[3]

Another way to describe these ideas is to imagine a documentary. Try to visualise a documentary about Australia. It could include pictures of Uluru, the Sydney Opera House, lots of footage of cuddly koalas and kangaroos, great expanses of the red dirt of a sunburnt country and possibly some shots of Bondi beach. While you would probably learn a lot from this documentary, a documentary about Australia is not Australia itself. A documentary cannot completely cover all the aspects of Australia or even begin to address its contradictions and ambiguities. A documentary can show you some of the sights and sounds of Australia and give you some powerful impressions, but it would not compare to the actual experience of travelling in Australia. Regardless of the skill of the director in filming the documentary or how 'real' it is, a documentary about Australia can never be Australia itself.[4]

Similarly, a documentary or a story about you would not be the same as you yourself. Even if that documentary lasted a million hours and included lots of interviews with people who know you best and included your most private and relevant details, the documentary still would not be you. It would be full of gaps and inconsistencies and contradictions.[5] It would be a thin replication of the thick and rich story that is you. Therefore, there is a huge difference between who you are and any story or documentary anyone could ever make about you. All stories and documentaries tend to be very biased as they can only show you a very small part of the big picture. In addition, the documentary will be biased by the film director who will choose the 'best' of hundreds of hours of footage to fit into a 45-minute documentary. To really get a feel for this, think about the person you love the most in this world. Which would you want to spend time with: the living person or the documentary about that person?[6]

In a sense, we all have a powerful story or documentary about ourselves called 'This is who I am'. Unfortunately, it is put together by our 'thinking mind', which is much more biased than any human documentary director could ever be. The thinking mind selects a few pivotal memories out of an entire lifetime of experience and edits them together with a few related opinions and judgements from you and others in your life, and then says, 'This is you.' The problem is, when we watch that video or hear that story we forget that it is just a documentary or just a story. Instead we let that video or story totalise us, and we believe we are that video/story. But in the same way that the documentary about Australia was not Australia, a story about you is not you. Your ideas about the sort of person you are, your self-image, your self-esteem, are nothing more than thoughts and memories. They are not you.[7] No story, film, or picture can fully represent you in totality. They will always be thin representations of who you are.

In addition, Narrative Therapy highlights that you are the expert on you. No one else knows you as well as you know yourself. No one else is privy to every thought, feeling and experience you have ever had – only you are. This stands in stark contrast to the thin descriptions of people's identities and actions that are often created by others. For example, parents and teachers often have the power of definition in children's lives and a child may become known as the 'attention seeker' or the 'trouble maker'. Health professionals often have this power of definition in the lives of people who consult them and Rose may become labelled as the 'generalised anxiety disorder'. These labels can have real effects on how individuals see themselves and also how others view them.

Can you identify any stories about yourself, and what they would be named?

_____

_____

_____

_____

_____

_____

Dominant stories have real effects

The story of Rose 'panicking over nothing' not only affects her in the present but also has implications for her future actions. For example, if Rose is asked to answer some questions in front of the managers in her job or go on an adventure camping trip her decision will be influenced by the dominant story she has about panicking in tricky situations. Rose would probably be more likely to agree to do these things when influenced by her story of being 'calm under pressure' rather than if she had a dominant story of being 'easily stressed and highly anxious'. Consequently, the meanings Rose gives to these events are not neutral in their effects on her life. They will constitute and shape her life in the future. The stories we have about our lives shape our lives and are essential to the type of life we lead.[8]

The social context

The reality that Rose's story of 'panicking over nothing' has been reinforced by her family and friends reflects the fact that stories are never produced in isolation from outside influences.[9]

We do not live in a vacuum and so we are influenced by the broader stories of the society and culture in which we live. As we said in Chapter 3, society is like an umbrella over all of us. Society is made up of a number of things, including media, school and other educational institutions, church, legal systems, the government, and the Internet. This broader social context affects the interpretations and meanings that Rose would give to events. The context of gender, class, race, culture and sexual preference may also have powerful effects on the meanings Rose gives her life. For example, if Rose was subjected to abuse then it would make perfect sense that she should feel anxious as this would be her body's way of telling her she is unsafe. It would be inappropriate to treat this anxiety without addressing the social context of abuse within which Rose was living.

Sometimes society can seem to push some 'dominant ideas', as if they were facts or the truth. When we look at these ideas closely and stop taking them for granted we can be very surprised to see that they are not 'the truth' but just ideas that are pushed by some very powerful people or institutions in our society. For example, the idea that women's stressors are less stressful than those of men. Is this the truth? Is it a fact? Many messages people get from school, television and other significant sources suggest that women are the 'weaker sex'. There is also the idea that the stress provided by running a home and family is not as stressful as the work of men who tend to have greater status, power and position in relation to women. In addition, there may be taken-for-granted assumptions that women's stressors are internal whereas men's stressors are external.[10] These taken-for-granted beliefs and assumptions that masquerade as truth or reality can have real effects on people's lives. Through a process of questioning, Narrative Therapy seeks to unmask these taken-for-granted beliefs and assumptions.

What are some of the taken-for-granted ideas about women in our society?

_____

_____

_____

_____

_____

What are some of the taken-for-granted ideas about men in our society?

_____

_____

_____

_____

_____

Stories about ourselves

Narrative Therapy is based on the idea that it is through the stories people have about their own lives and the lives of others that they make sense of their experience. Not only do these stories determine the meaning a person gives to experience but these stories largely determine which aspects of experience people select out for expression. For example, with Narrative Therapy a client may move from being influenced by a story dominated by anxiety and stress to a less problem-saturated and more preferred story. Specific types of questions are asked in order to create a context that is non-labelling and non-pathologising, and focuses on possibilities that already exist.[11]

Far from being simplistic, narrative counselling is based on the understanding that problems are manufactured in a social, cultural and political context. From the narrative perspective, each person is born into a cultural context and problems float within this context. The problems we encounter are multi-sourced, they are developed over a long period of time, and they come together through the medium of human language to construct and produce our experience.[12]

Story framework in therapy

The narrative approach is not a step-by-step process. This model is based on the premise that questions don't access experience, they generate it. We are reminded of this each time one of our questions is met by a long pause, after which a person says, 'I have never thought of this before . . .' or 'I didn't know this until you asked that question'. We think it is not just that the person did not know it – we think it had never been so until the question and the person came together to constitute it that way.[13] This is why maintaining a stance of curiosity and asking questions to which you do not know the answers are crucial for a narrative therapist.

The following framework was proposed by Linell and Cora as a suggestion of a general narrative progression from past through the present to the future.[14] However, the steps are not a formula and often occur out of order or concurrently, just like in a story.

- The history of the problem.
- How the problem is affecting the person's life.
- How the person has managed, even occasionally or in a small way, not to let this problem completely overwhelm them.

- What the person's ability to challenge the problem on such occasions might tell them and other people about themselves.
- How the person can continue to use these personal qualities or strengths to challenge the problem.
- How the person's life might be different if they continue to do this.
- What the person predicts for themselves in the future based on their successes and what sympathetic others might predict for them.
- What kind of person the person is in the process of becoming and what others may say about this.
- How the person is going to update others in their life about their new story.
- How the person is going to celebrate their achievements.

A short story for you

To get a small taste of narrative, answer the following questions regarding your experiences with stress and/or anxiety. Take as much time as you need to think about your answers.

What is the impact of stress/anxiety on your life?

_____

_____

_____

_____

_____

_____

What are some of the views held within our society about people who experience stress/anxiety?

_____

_____

_____

_____

_____

How has stress impacted on your view of yourself?

_____

_____

_____

_____

_____

If stress/anxiety were to continue to dominate your life, how would this influence your future experience of yourself?

_____

_____

_____

_____

_____

Think of a time when in some small way you have been able to stand up to stress/anxiety and have stopped it pushing you around. Write about this event below.

_____

_____

_____

_____

_____

What qualities, skills or abilities did it take for you to resist stress in this way?

_____

_____

_____

_____

_____

How can you use these qualities, skills, abilities or strategies in the future to continue challenging stress/anxiety?

_____

_____

_____

_____

_____

Stress and anxiety can dominate our lives and make it hard for us to see how we have resisted its tricks and traps. Think back through your life to other times when you were able to outsmart stress and anxiety, and describe what happened.

_____

_____

_____

_____

_____

If you were to continue to challenge stress/anxiety in this way, how would your life be different?

_____

_____

_____

_____

_____

Think of someone who is special to you and knows you well. What would they predict for your life if they were made aware of your successes over stress and anxiety?

_____

_____

_____

_____

_____

What kind of person are you in the process of becoming, and what would your special person/s say about this?

_____

_____

_____

_____

_____

How are you going to 'catch up' the significant people in your life about your new story? What events will you tell them about so that they can appreciate you are no longer being tricked and trapped by stress/anxiety?

_____

_____

_____

_____

_____

How are you going to celebrate your achievements? Are you going to have some kind of ritual or ceremony and who are the important people you will invite to be an audience to your new story?

_____

_____

_____

_____

_____

How did you find these questions? Did they make you think in ways that you had not thought before? Perhaps some of the questions sounded strange and maybe they were difficult to answer because they were asking you to think the unthought. This is normal. We have used many of these narrative ideas and questions in our group work with people who have experienced stress and anxiety.[15,16] Below we have provided some explanations of the questions and included some answers given by other people we have worked with.

Q: WHAT IS THE IMPACT OF STRESS/ ANXIETY ON YOUR LIFE?

A: This question accesses the effects of stress/anxiety (the problem) on your life. Some of the effects include physical feelings of anxiety, loneliness, sleeplessness, making you question your value and worth, making you obnoxious to others, making people reject you because you are too needy; it drains and exhausts you, it has physical symptoms, it creates suicidal ideas, it breaks up your family. It has eroded your self-confidence, feelings of self-worth and your sense of humour.

Q: WHAT ARE SOME OF THE VIEWS HELD WITHIN OUR SOCIETY ABOUT PEOPLE WHO EXPERIENCE STRESS/ANXIETY?

A: This question unpacks the taken-for-granted assumptions that have become ingrained or widely accepted within our culture and masquerade as 'reality'. White Western culture has a very narrow definition of what 'success' is. As we outlined in Chapter 3, our comparing and competitive ways can be traced back to primitive times and were a matter of life and death back then. In modern times they are certainly not a matter of life and death, but sometimes we are tricked into acting as if they are. Our quest to be smarter, richer, thinner and more successful than others promises to lead us to contentment and calmness but more often leads to stress and anxiety.

Consequently, Narrative Therapy suggests it is crucial for us to question the taken-for-granted beliefs that may be pushing us around when we are feeling stressed and anxious. Society's messages may include that the individual is blameworthy, at fault, hopeless, inadequate and crazy. Society situates the fault within the individual and not the context. People think you are a 'stress-head', 'worry-wart' or 'misery guts'.

Q: HOW HAS STRESS/ANXIETY IMPACTED ON YOUR VIEW OF YOURSELF?

A: This question accesses the effect of the problem on you. When problems are present, 'thin descriptions' are often reached about a person's actions and identity. 'Thin descriptions' leave little space for the complexities and contradictions of life. They don't let people articulate their own particular meanings of their actions and the context within which they occurred. Often, thin descriptions of people's identities and actions are created by others. For example, parents and teachers often have the power of definition in children's lives and health professionals often have this power in the lives of people who consult them. Sometimes people come to understand their own actions through thin descriptions and these lead to thin conclusions, which have many negative effects.

Thin conclusions are often expressed as a truth about the person who is struggling with the anxiety/stress and this has negative effects on their identity. The person experiencing the anxiety/stress may be understood to be 'weak', a 'scaredy-cat' or a 'worry-wart'. These 'thin conclusions' drawn from problem-saturated stories disempower people because they are described in terms of inadequacies, disabilities, dysfunctions or weaknesses.[17] People we have worked with have indicated that stress makes them believe they are weak, inadequate, broken, not like other people, isolated and the only one not coping.

This question also 'externalises' the problem. This means the problem is spoken of as if it were a distinct entity or even a personality in its own right rather than part of the person. This is based on the idea that the problem is the problem, as opposed to the person being the problem.[18] Questions are asked about the influence of the problem on the person, on their relationships with others and on their view of themselves. Additionally, questions are asked about the person's influence over the problem. Sometimes children are asked to draw what the stress/anxiety looks like. This is a useful externalising technique that can work for adults too.

Q: IF STRESS/ANXIETY WERE TO CONTINUE TO DOMINATE YOUR LIFE, HOW WOULD THIS INFLUENCE YOUR FUTURE EXPERIENCE OF YOURSELF?

A: This question asks you to consider if you are ready to make changes. People we have worked with gave the following responses: I would feel fearful, a failure, depressed, helpless, hopeless, useless, full of blame and I would not want to continue with life like this.

Q: THINK OF A TIME, WHEN IN SOME SMALL WAY YOU HAVE BEEN ABLE TO STAND UP TO STRESS/ANXIETY AND HAVE STOPPED IT PUSHING YOU AROUND.

A: This question accesses 'unique outcomes'. Unique outcomes are small events that contradict the 'dominant' or 'problem' story. It is assumed that stress/anxiety will never be 100 per cent successful in claiming a person's life. These become the foundation for the alternative/preferred story and allow the person to recognise and develop agency (agency refers to the person's ability to act to produce preferred outcomes in their own life).[19] For example, a unique outcome for someone struggling with stress and anxiety may include going to the letterbox, answering the phone, disclosing to a friend that they experience stress/anxiety, saying 'no' when they don't want to do something, driving the car, or being able to laugh at a joke. A unique outcome can be anything that the problem would not like, anything that does not fit with the dominant (or problem) story. Unique outcomes can be an action, a plan, a feeling, a statement, a quality, a dream, a thought, a belief, a commitment or an ability.[20]

Becoming reconnected with your sense of humour, even for a short time, can be a strong sign of resistance toward stress/anxiety.[21] Alternative stories become 'richly described' when they are made up of many unique outcomes. Alternative stories can reduce the influence of the anxiety/stress and create new possibilities for living.[22] Sykes has compared searching for unique outcomes to looking for gold. She suggested that the work of a narrative therapist can be likened to that of a gold prospector, who pans for gold in a stream long since abandoned by other prospectors. The prospector slowly and meticulously sifts through sand, patiently extracting tiny flakes until she/he has amassed an astonishing mound of precious gold.[23] In the same way, the narrative therapist works steadfastly and carefully to reveal the unique outcomes that will support the preferred story for the client.

Q: WHAT QUALITIES, SKILLS OR ABILITIES DID IT TAKE FOR YOU TO RESIST STRESS IN THIS WAY?

A: This question is inviting the person to reflect on the meanings of the unique outcome as a way of cementing the unique outcome in its importance to the alternative story. A person may identify that it took courage, strength or quick thinking to resist stress/anxiety. This question also encourages the person to realise their agency: it was not just luck or a fluke, it was their action that led to the positive outcome.[24] One of the most crucial aspects of the alternative story is that it is identified by the person who is re-authoring their life. They are not just any alternative stories, but stories that are chosen by the person seeking counselling as stories by which they would like to live their lives.[25]

Q: HOW CAN YOU USE THESE QUALITIES, SKILLS, ABILITIES AND STRATEGIES IN THE FUTURE TO CONTINUE CHALLENGING STRESS/ANXIETY?

A: This question gets you to consider how you can continue your resistance to the stress/anxiety. This question also works to reinforce that the emerging alternative story needs to be nurtured and protected against the ongoing tricks and traps of stress/anxiety. By drawing on your long history of successful strategies to resist stress/anxiety we strengthen the knowledge that these skills and abilities have not been newly acquired but have a long history.[26] In addition, you are asked to reconnect with skills and strategies you have used in the past, such as relaxation techniques, accessing support systems and engaging in self-care strategies. This is important because stress/anxiety works to undermine self-confidence and self-worth.[27]

Q: STRESS AND ANXIETY CAN DOMINATE OUR LIVES AND MAKE IT HARD FOR US TO SEE HOW WE HAVE RESISTED ITS TRICKS AND TRAPS. THINK BACK THROUGH YOUR LIFE TO OTHER TIMES WHEN YOU WERE ABLE TO OUTSMART STRESS/ANXIETY AND DESCRIBE WHAT HAPPENED BELOW.

A: Again, this question is asking about the history of unique outcomes that may have been ignored, overlooked or disqualified.

Q: IF YOU WERE TO CONTINUE TO CHALLENGE STRESS/ANXIETY IN THIS WAY, HOW WOULD YOUR LIFE BE DIFFERENT?

A: This question gets you to think about your future and what is important for you and what you want for your life. It accesses goals and values.

Q: THINK OF SOMEONE WHO IS SPECIAL TO YOU AND KNOWS YOU WELL. WHAT WOULD THEY PREDICT FOR YOUR LIFE IF THEY WERE MADE AWARE OF YOUR SUCCESSES OVER STRESS/ANXIETY?

A: This question accesses the important people in your life. One of the main tricks of stress/anxiety is to isolate you and disconnect you from important relationships. This question seeks to richly describe your life by accessing memories of events from your special person when you displayed certain abilities, qualities and skills. Through this type of question an alternative account of your identity can be generated and the significant relationships of your life can be explored.[28]

Q: WHAT KIND OF PERSON ARE YOU IN THE PROCESS OF BECOMING AND WHAT WOULD YOUR SPECIAL PERSON/S SAY ABOUT THIS?

A: This question gets you to reflect upon the new stress/anxiety-free identity you are developing and to also evaluate what special others would think about these developments in your life.

Q: HOW ARE YOU GOING TO 'CATCH UP' THE SIGNIFICANT PEOPLE IN YOUR LIFE ABOUT YOUR NEW STORY? WHAT EVENTS WILL YOU TELL THEM ABOUT SO THAT THEY CAN APPRECIATE YOU ARE NO LONGER BEING TRICKED AND TRAPPED BY STRESS/ANXIETY?

A: This question again focuses on you reconnecting with significant people in your life. This provides a contrast to many current cultural practices that encourage individualisation and disconnection of people from one another.[29] In addition, each time you catch people up on the new developments in your life you are reinforcing your preferred story by performing it over and over again to a supportive audience specially selected by you. Gaining an audience to unique outcomes is a powerful step to use to shape your own life.[30]

Q: HOW ARE YOU GOING TO CELEBRATE YOUR ACHIEVEMENTS? ARE YOU GOING TO HAVE SOME KIND OF RITUAL OR CEREMONY AND WHO ARE THE IMPORTANT PEOPLE YOU WILL INVITE TO BE AN AUDIENCE TO YOUR NEW STORY?

A: This question introduces the idea of rituals and ceremonies to mark and celebrate your journey away from the stress/anxiety story towards your new and preferred version of life. In addition, this can also involve deliberate decisions to exclude people who have been pivotal in keeping the dominant/stress/anxiety story alive.[31] By privileging those people who are deemed to be supportive of your new story you are creating a context that will nourish your new preferred way of being.

So the plot thickens and the journey continues!

In conclusion, Narrative Therapy is a respectful, non-blaming approach to stress/anxiety that recognises people are the experts in their own lives. It holds that the stress/anxiety is the problem and the person is not the problem. Narrative Therapy also assumes that people have many abilities, qualities, values and skills that will assist them to change their relationship with the stress/anxiety in their lives.

This chapter in no way covers the constantly evolving body of knowledge and skills that has come to be known as Narrative Therapy. Hopefully, it provides you with a 'travel brochure' that may encourage you to explore further if you wish. The journey provided by Narrative Therapy has no right way, just many possible directions. These directions are chosen by you. The road you choose represents the alternative story to the stress/anxiety story. It is not just any road or any alternative story, it is the story by which you would like to live your life. If you would like to explore this approach further, some references are provided in the 'Further resources' section at the end of this book.

TRAVEL REMINDERS

Here are some reminders from this chapter. You may want to copy them and make them into a reminder card to place in your diary or wallet, or even on the fridge or a mirror at home.

- **We create stories about our lives to make sense of our experiences and to make our lives meaningful.**
- **We have lots of stories happening at the same time.**
- **No story can fully represent you.**
- **You are the expert on yourself.**
- **You are not the problem – the problem is the problem!**
- **Dominant stories and social context can shape our lives.**
- **Questions help us to understand these influences and generate new experience.**
- **Narrative Therapy provides an alternative story to the stress/anxiety story.**

TRAVEL DIARY

RELATIONSHIPS, ACCEPTANCE AND COMPASSION

> For a long time it had seemed to me
> that life was about to begin - real
> life. But there was always some
> obstacle in the way, something
> to be gotten through first, some
> unfinished business, time still to
> be served, a debt to be paid. Then
> life would begin. At last it dawned
> on me that these obstacles were my
> life.

–Alfred D'Souza

This chapter is about relationships: your relationship to stress and anxiety, your relationship to significant others in your life and most importantly your relationship to yourself. Your relationship with stress/anxiety is probably similar to other relationships in your life. At times it feels as if you can co-exist together without too many problems and you are able to be the person you want to be. At other times it feels as if the stress/anxiety is trying to wreak havoc in your life. Notice the common denominator here is feelings, and they tend to change a bit like the weather. Sometimes they are stormy, sometimes calm, sometimes predictable and sometimes not very predictable at all. Feelings tend to be fairly fickle and that's why they are not the best foundation to base your actions on, especially in relationships.

Through this chapter we will address how changing the way you relate to the stress and anxiety and how you treat yourself can have a positive flow-on effect to other significant relationships in your life. We will also touch on some simple ideas to build richness, abundance and loving-kindness into your relationships.

Acceptance

Acceptance refers to taking what comes our way, and it is a type of readiness to recognise the way things are.[1] Acceptance is the opposite to pretending, ignoring, enduring, rationalising, denying or other forms of running from reality. It is also the necessary first step in making change. Change needs to be responsive to reality.[2] Acceptance means fully opening yourself to your present reality and acknowledging how it is, right in this present moment. It can also mean letting go of the struggle, as it is in this present moment.[3] Taking action can be far more effective when you start from a position of acceptance. Much time and energy is wasted struggling and fighting with thoughts and feelings of stress and anxiety. When these thoughts and feelings are accepted instead of fought, then helpful action can be taken. Meaningful actions are guided by your values and lead to a rich and fulfilling life.[4]

Acceptance does not mean passivity, resigning yourself to it, admitting defeat, putting up with it, giving up, getting through it, tolerating it, or grinning and bearing it.[5] Acceptance is about how things are, not how they were, should have been or might have been. Neither is it about how you wanted it to be, planned it would be or hoped it would be. Acceptance involves active skills that will help you respond with kindness, compassion and gentleness towards yourself when anxieties, stress, worries, fears, panic and other emotional and psychological pain appear. The concept is to accept what you are already experiencing anyway, and thereby disarm the struggle you are having with unwanted thoughts and feelings. As you learn to let go and accept, your anxious suffering tends to decrease.[6]

Write down a thought that you would like to work on accepting.

_____

_____

_____

_____

Write down a feeling that you would like to work on accepting.

_____

_____

_____

_____

ACCEPTING STRESS AND ANXIETY

Acceptance sounds easy but the invitations to avoid the feelings, thoughts, sensations and images associated with our stress and anxiety can be irresistible at times. As we have discussed in previous chapters, excessive avoidance of stress and anxiety is the real problem that is responsible for turning worries, fears and anxieties into life-limiting issues. Avoidance of fear and anxiety can include using substances such as drugs and alcohol to minimise the occurrence of such feelings or avoiding people, places and activities that may lead to anxious feelings. It may also involve running away from situations where you experience uncomfortable feelings. The basic purpose of all these behaviours is the same; that is, to make anxiety and stress disappear. Avoidance is the thread that binds all anxiety problems together.[7]

Being able to catch these urges, feelings, thoughts or judgements and name them for what they are, and learning to sit with uncomfortable feelings, can provide an antidote to the avoidance and a pathway to acceptance.[8] Acceptance can mean acknowledging that you will never be fully rid of stress and anxiety so instead you develop a different relationship to them. As we said in Chapter 7, sometimes re-storying or re-authoring your relationship with the stress and anxiety can be a powerful way of changing how you respond to it. The following relaxation exercise helps you to visualise your relationship with anxiety in a different way.

TRAINING YOURSELF TO ACCEPT EXERCISE

Get into your relaxation position and start your deep, regular breathing. Imagine that you are the driver of a train called 'your life' and you have chosen the correct tracks that will lead to a rich and fulfilling life via your

values. You have started moving and you're looking forward to an enjoyable journey. Suddenly, there is an unscheduled stop to pick up some 'trouble-making' passengers such as scary images, thoughts and judgements that you view as monsters. These passengers have brought their friends along, which include stress, anxiety, fear and worries. You try to pretend they are not on board your train but they are noisy and obnoxious. You banish them to the carriage right at the back of the train but these passengers are sneaky and persistent and they try to trick you into driving the train the way they want. They shout things like: 'Watch out, don't try that, it's dangerous', 'What if something goes wrong?', 'It's no use, you will embarrass yourself, you will get it wrong.' You try to reason with them, to quiet them and finally you lock the door to that carriage and frantically try to get back to driving the train.

As you are looking in the rear view mirror to keep an eye on the unwanted passengers, you drive off your chosen track. Only after a considerable time do you realise you are on the wrong track and that you are lost. You decide to stop the train and focus on controlling the passengers. You move to the back of the train and unleash a tirade on them: 'Why don't you leave me alone, I hate you, I am sick of you, just go away.' As you are facing the back of the train, trying to sort out the other unhelpful passengers, anxiety has snuck into the driver's seat of your life and you have become a passenger. Instead of staying focused on the road ahead and your real destination, anxiety is making all the decisions.

You are now at a crossroads in the track and you have a choice. You can stay in the passenger seat of your life, hooked up in strategies to keep the passengers in order, or you can politely take back the driver's seat from anxiety and get back on track. You have realised that these passengers have no power unless you give it to them. You have realised that you need to focus on the track ahead and move towards your values. The passengers are still there, you cannot ban them from the train or control them, but you can control the way you react to them. You can make sure you take them along for your journey, not theirs.

How was this exercise? Was it useful to externalise stress, anxiety and worries in this way?

_____

_____

_____

_____

This exercise was taken from Forsyth and Eifert and was developed to illustrate that anxiety can be a monster crippling your life or it can be a temporary experience that comes and goes pretty much by itself.[9] It is all a matter of how you view it and respond to it. You cannot control the passengers who ride along with you on your life train. What you can control is how you respond to them and whether you keep on moving toward your values. The stress and anxiety passengers will take every opportunity to steer you off course. They will try to convince you that the journey is too hard, not worth it and you don't feel like it anymore. You can't choose what feelings, thoughts, urges and fears travel with you but you can control the direction of the train.

In the next exercise we would like to take the life train metaphor a bit further to try to make stress and anxiety better travel companions. Instead of monsters and demons we would like you to visualise them as children. Although stress and anxiety feel like monsters, they are more like kids. Like most kids, they respond better to loving-kindness than to reprimand, punishment or nagging. If you don't have children, try to imagine what it might be like to have children or imagine a child you know (and hopefully like!). Maybe if we were to approach our stress and anxiety with kindness and compassion we would be better able to accept them and move with them instead of against them. Compassion and kindness could take the power out of stress and anxiety.

CARING FOR YOUR ANXIETY CHILDREN EXERCISE

Get into your relaxation position and start your deep, regular breathing. Again imagine that you are the driver of a train called 'your life' and you have chosen the correct tracks that will lead to a rich and fulfilling life via your values. You have started moving and you're looking forward to an enjoyable journey. You turn around and see your two-year-old 'anxiety child' out of her child seat and demanding attention and power at the same time. How are you going to respond?

You feel defeated, provoked, challenged, annoyed and irritated all at the same time. The 'authoritarian' parenting style would demand that you control, punish, scold, chastise, struggle, nag, shout, smack and scream at your anxiety child to make her do what you want. When you do this your child experiences negative energy as she takes one punishment after the next, but she learns nothing. In addition your anxiety child wants to respond to your behaviour by listening less, resisting, retaliating and rebelling against you and your behaviours. So you are now caught in a vicious cycle with your tantruming anxiety child. The more you try to control and threaten her the more she resists and the bigger her tantrum becomes. Many research studies have shown that these strategies are poor ways to encourage more appropriate behaviours in children. Parents end up feeling frustrated, sad and tired and the kids go on being kids, but now with exhausted, frustrated and angry parents.

The 'authoritative' parenting style offers a kind but firm approach for parents. They don't resort to lashing out, fighting or punishing behaviour simply because their child is misbehaving. They avert that first impulse to react negatively and instead respond with patience and calm. They realise they are bigger, stronger, wiser and need to act with kindness. They see their child as a part of them. They respond in a way that reflects their wish for that child to know kindness and love. They also act as their child's most important role model, they act in the way they want their child to act and guide the child in directions the parent wants to go. These directions are best for the child too. By taking actions that seem counterintuitive you can embrace your tantruming anxiety child with calm and kindness. You will be amazed at how quickly the fight moves out of your anxiety child and is replaced by calm and stillness. This way of parenting has been shown to be highly effective by many research studies.[10]

Now is the time to choose the relationship you want to have with your anxiety child. If you scream and struggle your anxiety child will learn to copy you and will fight back just as hard. You would not let your child sidetrack you and get you hooked into unproductive antics. You would do what you set out to do when you left home, and that means taking your anxiety child with you. Perhaps it's

time to be firm but kind; after all, your stress and anxiety is part of you. Perhaps it is time to drive into life with your anxiety child. [11]

How was that exercise? Was it easier to accept your stress and anxiety when you visualised it as child?

_____

_____

_____

_____

_____

_____

Valuing relationships

Parenting can also provide a good example of your train journey being guided by values. Value-focused living is a journey not a destination. Values are not about achieving outcomes. Most parents want the very best for their children and do what they can to make that happen. Yet engaging the value of parenting is no guarantee that your children will be healthy and safe and grow up to be responsible or functional adults. However, not knowing the outcome for their children does not stand in the way of parents who value parenting trying to be the very best parents they can be.

Unlike goals, values are lifelong journeys. Values are like the compass that directs us towards what is important in our lives. Goals are the stopovers on the map, places you plan to visit as you travel towards your values. For example, reaching your goal of reading to your children every night of the week does not fulfil your value of being a good parent. Values such as being a good parent are ongoing commitments that are reflected in everyday and every moment actions. A value is never completed and ticked off a list like a goal.

The same is true of other values that have outcomes which are largely uncertain. For example, love relationships, friendships, health, career and financial stability. Values focus your attention on the here and now, which is the process. If you choose values exclusively on the basis of outcomes, you will be waiting a very long time to see them and you will be disappointed if the outcome is not 'successful' in the way you expected. For example, achieving the goal of getting married and staying together until death do you part, is not the same as living the value of being a devoted loving partner on a moment-to-moment basis throughout the relationship. Again, values are about the process or the journey, not like goals, which are about the outcome or destination.

CHARLOTTE'S STORY

Charlotte was arranging a birthday party for her son, Max. Charlotte was anxious that the house would be clean, the food would be fantastic and plentiful and that all her four children would look perfect and behave well on the day. Charlotte had started worrying six weeks before the event and this was making her stressed and snappy with her children. Charlotte began to realise that even if the party was a wonderful success, it did not justify how she was treating her children now. She realised the end did not justify the means so instead she started focusing on having fun with her children as they enjoyed the process of planning and organising the party together.

In relationships, the ends definitely do not justify the means. For example, take your relationship with anxiety. The anxiety may be trying to get you to avoid social situations. You may decide to get the upper hand on anxiety and you force yourself to attend social occasions despite the anxiety. That is, you tolerate the anxiety feelings even though they are distressing you. In a sense you are still avoiding the feelings because you are still struggling with the feelings, are distressed by them and are hoping that they will go away. This is the difference between tolerance and acceptance. With acceptance you may be experiencing the feelings as uncomfortable and unpleasant but you are not distressed by them. Imagine this distinction in your love relationship. It would mean tolerating the people you love when they are present and hoping that they go away soon, while constantly checking to see if they have gone yet. Now contrast this with totally and completely accepting them as they are, warts and all, and being willing to have them around for as long as they choose to stay.[12]

Realising and accepting that we don't have control over the outcomes in many important areas of our lives, such as parenting and relationships, can be quite anxiety-provoking. Do you remember the 'three buckets' exercise in Chapter 3? This exercise illustrated how we do not have as much control over others as ourselves, and may be helpful in dealing with this anxiety.

Accepting and stopping the struggle

A feature common to people struggling with anxiety is the propensity to be hard on themselves. The people we have worked with feel they are weak or flawed or broken in some way because the anxiety is running their lives. This tendency to 'whip themselves' is not written about in many books but is certainly a strong feature of anxiety issues that can make the whole experience worse.

It is a message our mind sends us frequently, always some version of the 'I'm not good enough' story. This makes sense given the evolution of the mind we described in Chapter 5. The mind evolved to help us survive by constantly highlighting our weaknesses so we could improve and thereby contribute more than the next person in the clan. By constantly comparing us to others, our 'thinking self' strived to keep us alive by avoiding rejection by the clan. (Remember the 'thinking self' is the part of you that thinks, judges, plans, compares, creates, imagines, visualises, analyses, remembers daydreams and fantasises.)[13] However, living with a mind that continually identifies the ways in which you are 'not good enough' can lead you to feel unsuccessful, unattractive, unlovable, unworthy, unacceptable, inadequate and incompetent to name a few.

ELIZA'S STORY

Eliza is 32 years old, has three degrees and is in a highly paid job. She is in a relationship with Peter but she is constantly anxious that he will leave her. She had a long-term relationship in the past which ended suddenly when her partner found someone else. This made Eliza feel as if she was 'not good enough'. She now pretends to be what she thinks Peter would like her to be so he won't leave her. Peter is unhappy because he believes Eliza does not trust him enough to let him in to see the 'real' Eliza. Peter is thinking of leaving the relationship because it makes him feel as if he is 'not good enough'. They both believe that their problem is caused by low self-esteem.

The problem with self-esteem

Problems are often labelled as being caused by 'low self-esteem'. Consequently, as the label implies, the solution is to get high self-esteem. Ironically, the solution implies again that you are inadequate or deficient in some way. In *A Handbook for Constructive Living*, Reynolds wrote that if he were the devil he would invent the idea that you need self-esteem before you can do anything, then he would not offer any genuine way to develop self-esteem apart from doing something well.[14]

Think of how someone has described you and write that description on the lines below.

_____

_____

_____

_____

_____

Think of how you would describe yourself and write that on the lines below.

_____

_____

_____

_____

_____

Which description is more positive? Which description do you believe to be true? What conclusions would you draw about your ability to judge?

_____

_____

_____

_____

_____

_____

Self-esteem is an opinion you have about what kind of person you are. High self-esteem is a good opinion of yourself and low self-esteem is a bad opinion of yourself. Therefore, self-esteem is a group of thoughts about the type of person you are. It is not the truth, it is not a fact, it is just an opinion, a story. Remember what we learnt in Chapter 7: that the stories we have about ourselves can never fully encompass all the complexities and ambiguities about who we are. We all have a story or documentary about ourselves called 'This is who I am'. The problem is that when we watch that video or read that story we forget that it is just a documentary or just a story.

Instead we let that video or story totalise us, we believe we are that documentary/story. Your ideas about the sort of person you are, your self-image, and your self-esteem are nothing more than thoughts and memories. They are not you.[15] No story, film or picture can fully represent you in totality. They will always be thin representations of who you are and they are always influenced by the broader context of culture and society. Consequently, self-esteem is a highly subjective judgement that our 'thinking self' makes about us as a person.[16]

So if the solution is high self-esteem, how do we go about getting it? In a sense we have to convince our 'thinking mind' that we are an okay person by means of justifying, reasoning and negotiation. The issue here is that you have to constantly argue or prove you are 'a good person'. This can be exhausting and time-consuming as for each bit of evidence you provide for your argument of being good, your thinking mind will probably provide an equally convincing piece of evidence for the opposing position. It is as if you are caught up supporting your position in a court case against a lawyer who is just as determined as you to win. The dilemma is that if your self-esteem is low you feel awful, but if it is high you are continually working to keep it there. The only way to drop this no-win situation is to let go of judging yourself as a person.[17] When we do this we are left with self-acceptance and self-compassion.

Self-acceptance

Self-acceptance means accepting yourself as valuable for your very humanness and being all right with who you are. It means recognising that you do not need to earn your worth through things such as your achievements, appearance, possessions, qualifications or job. It means accepting yourself with all your perceived flaws and shortcomings, as being as inherently valuable as any other person. Finally, it means believing that you are worthwhile just because you are human and, like everyone else, you are just trying to live.[18]

The Japanese Morita and Naikan therapies suggest that we are what we are right now, and we need to accept this as it is. Effort should be focused on what needs doing right now, and not on some perfect future.[19] Constructive Living is the therapy that was derived from these two Japanese therapies and it too focuses on acceptance. Constructive Living suggests that part of a greater principle of accepting reality as it is means accepting yourself just the way you are, including all that you do and don't do. Getting caught in negative evaluations and unsympathetic non-acceptance of the way you are now will cause you unnecessary suffering. It further suggests we are just fine as we are.[20]

LUCIA'S STORY

Lucia had teenage twin girls named Sophia and Helen. She found it extremely easy to be around Sophia as they had several interests in common and Sophia had many qualities that Lucia admired and appreciated. On the other hand, Lucia found Helen to be 'stubborn and opinionated' and they argued frequently.

Lucia began to notice that she was avoiding Helen as a way of decreasing the arguments. Lucia also started feeling guilty and bad about herself as a mother because of this avoidance. Then one day, by chance, another mother reflected to Lucia how proud she must be of Helen's 'strong character and determination' which had helped her overcome a very difficult situation at school. This 'off the cuff' remark helped Lucia view Helen's qualities with more flexibility. In addition, Lucia took committed action to spend extra quality time alone with Helen. Instead of running from the difficulty, she leaned into it. Lucia soon found she was able to enjoy her time with Helen more and more.

The following exercise is aimed at getting you to think about your own qualities differently. In Chapter 7 we talked about how our views of ourself are influenced by society and the other people in our lives. We also discussed how we often believe that an idea is the truth or a fact about us, when it is just an idea. We would like you to answer the following three questions.

YOUR QUALITIES EXERCISE

Write down the qualities you value and appreciate in yourself.

_____

_____

_____

_____

_____

_____

Write down the qualities you do not value or appreciate in yourself.

_____

_____

_____

_____

_____

_____

_____

Now rename or reframe the qualities you do not value or appreciate in yourself. For example, Helen's stubbornness became determination and strength of character.

_____

_____

_____

_____

Some people may find it difficult to identify their qualities as society sends us the message not to 'blow our own trumpet' or be egotistical. It is okay to be realistic about your positive qualities as well as your not-so-positive qualities. You may wish to ask others, who know you well and appreciate you, to add to your list. When you consider the qualities you don't appreciate in yourself, think about how your best friend would describe that quality. Also think about where you might have got the idea that it is not a good quality. Most qualities, and emotions for that matter, are neither good nor bad. Sometimes they work for us and sometimes they work against us.

For example, perfectionism can make a chef very good at their job, but if it is too extreme, it can make them inefficient because they don't get the food out on time. It is important to remember that our positives and negatives can be like two sides of the same coin. A strength such as being easy-going can also work against you at times and be interpreted as being unmotivated.[21] This exercise was designed to help you increase your psychological flexibility, which we discussed in Chapter 6. By being able to reframe your personal qualities more positively you may find it easier to move towards self-acceptance.

Another idea that may help with self-acceptance is the idea of the 'observing self' or the 'hidden observer' which we described in Chapter 6. As we explained, there are two parts to the human mind – the 'thinking self' or thinking mind and the observing self. The observing self is the part of us from which we observe feelings, thoughts and memories. This is the part of us that is able to 'step back' and observe these things while remaining separate from them. This part of us does not get hooked up in what our judgemental mind is telling us. You know that you are thinking because this part of you called the observing self is able to observe your thoughts. This is the same for your feelings and actions: you know you are feeling and doing because part of you is observing these things. The observing self enables our capacity for self-awareness.[22]

The observing self has many special qualities, including being the source of true acceptance. It observes everything you do and never judges you, and it cannot be improved upon in any way. The observing self has been there with you from birth and will be so until death, and is unchanging. It is always there, whether we forget about it or don't even know about it. It is not made of physical matter and it cannot be hurt or damaged in any way. This last point can be very reassuring for people who have felt damaged by their stress and anxiety, and especially people who have been abused in some way as a child or an adult.

Remember, this part of your mind cannot be hurt or damaged in any way. People who have been abused often experience a great deal of anxiety. As we said in Chapter 7, all problems can only be understood in a social context, so if your anxiety is happening in a context of abuse then that anxiety is trying to keep you safe. Abuse or domestic violence is not okay and we would never suggest acceptance of this. However, to move forward you may need to accept the reality of your situation: you are in danger and need to take action to protect yourself or your children. The action taken may be to leave the relationship and you may have to accept many painful feelings and thoughts to do this. Acceptance and action often go together in this way.[23]

Again self-acceptance may be easier said than done. Reconnecting with your compassion and kindness can be useful steps towards self-acceptance.

Self-compassion

Compassion is sympathy for the suffering of others. To have compassion for others you must first notice their suffering and then feel warmth or caring and a desire to help in some way. Compassion also means that you offer understanding and kindness to others when they make mistakes or fail, rather than judging them harshly. Finally, when you feel compassion for another it reflects a recognition that suffering, imperfection and failure are part of the shared human experience.[24]

Self-compassion means you are kind and understanding towards yourself when faced by your personal failings, instead of mercilessly criticising and judging yourself. You may make changes in your life that fit with what is important to you because you care about yourself, not because you are unacceptable or worthless as you are. Having compassion for yourself means you accept and honour your humanness.[25] To develop compassion, it is helpful to cultivate your capacity for loving-kindness so it resembles that of a mother to her newborn child.[26]

The following exercise was adapted from an exercise by Forsyth and Eifert and provides a powerful way to get in touch with your sense of compassion.[27]

GIVING YOURSELF COMPASSION AND
KINDNESS EXERCISE

Get into your relaxation position and start your deep, regular breathing. Self-compassion and loving-kindness are gentle and soft. You can embrace your anxiety in the way you might hold something fragile like a newborn child, you can take care of yourself and your anxieties by giving yourself compassion and loving-kindness. We are going to reflect on the loving-kindness a mother shows her child. Even if you did not know your mother or did not get the type of loving mothering you deserved, you can give that to yourself now. A loving mother shows unconditional love, acceptance and compassion. She holds her child lovingly and tenderly, especially when that child is upset or sick.

Begin to imagine the feelings of being held, snug and secure in your mother's warm, soft arms. Imagine your mother's hand gently stroking your forehead and allow the energy of your mother's tender and adoring touch to radiate into you. Gently touch your own forehead now, and allow the energy of the love, tenderness and compassion that you should have received as a child to radiate through your own hand. You can take care of yourself, your anxieties and your pain by giving yourself compassion and kindness now. The kindness and compassion of the mothering you deserved is alive in your heart and hands right now. You can give that loving-kindness to yourself at any time you wish and in any place.

Kindness

Practising acts of kindness towards yourself and others is a behavioural antidote to anxiety and stress. It's a simple thing you can do to bring more peace and joy to your life. Kindness begets kindness and the power of kindness cannot be underestimated.[28] People cannot always get what they want or be who they wish to be. When we struggle with or deny this reality our suffering increases in the form of stress and self-hate. When this reality is accepted with compassion and kindness stress and anxiety are decreased.[29] Compassion and kindness are actions, not feelings.

The exercise below will give you some ideas about how to practise loving-kindness.

PRACTISING LOVING-KINDNESS EXERCISE

Be mindful of any chance you get throughout your day to act in kind and compassionate ways towards yourself and others. These acts of kindness could take many forms. Below are some examples.

- **Say please, thank you and you are welcome more often.**
- **Ask a shop assistant how they are going and really pay attention to the answer.**
- **Smile at a stranger.**
- **Ring a friend to tell them you are thinking of them.**
- **Send a relative a card to show your appreciation of them.**
- **Give a hug or kiss to a loved one.**
- **Give out five genuine compliments each day.**
- **Show understanding, compassion and forgiveness when you feel hurt and the urge to strike back.**
- **When you are thinking positive things about someone, let them know.**
- **Do something kind for yourself each day.**

Write down one small act of kindness you will do for yourself every day.

_____

_____

_____

_____

Engaging in these random acts of kindness can often lead to feeling more connected with others and more positive within yourself. It is important to take the time to look for moments when you can share, show care, offer gratitude or extend warmth. Similarly, look for opportunities to offer hope, love or a helping hand. Do this when you would rather shut down, cut off or explode. These are the moments when the benefits of practising loving-kindness through your actions are most needed and when they will benefit you and others the most.[30]

Some of the unexpected outcomes of acting with kindness can be an increased sense of peace, love and trust. You may find that people are drawn to you when you act with kindness. This way of being can only enrich your relationships. An exercise that our clients have found really useful as a way of reconnecting with positive feelings, such as kindness, is to make themselves a treasure chest.

MAKING A TREASURE CHEST EXERCISE
Find a box about the size of a shoebox. In this box, place all your precious mementos that trigger memories which have good feelings associated with them. (Make sure the memory is not ambiguous or confusing; for example, does not have both good and bad feelings associated with it.) These

treasures can include: special cards; invitations to special occasions; photos of happy occasions like holidays, weddings and birthdays; drawings from your children.

Once you have filled the box, spend time decorating your treasure chest in a way that best fits for you.

How did you find making a treasure chest?

_____

_____

_____

_____

This exercise serves a number of purposes:

- **Research has shown that our memories are encoded with feeling states. When we remember an occasion we usually re-experience the feelings associated with that place and time. In Chapter 4 we described how we don't have much control over feelings. This exercise offers one simple way to have a little bit of control over your feelings. By looking in your treasure chest you have real things to trigger good memories and hopefully good feelings.**
- **Many people find engaging in creative activities relaxing and fulfilling. They often enjoy the feelings of achievement they experience after finishing their project.**
- **This exercise promotes self-nurturing and self-care because you are taking time out to do something enjoyable for yourself.**
- **Other research has shown that if we focus on our actions our feelings will follow. Therefore, taking positive**

action to do something creative, self-nurturing and meaningful, such as making the treasure chest, should theoretically result in positive feelings.

- **Finally, this exercise can promote connection and loving-kindness towards yourself and others. For example, you may like to do the activity with a group of friends so you can exchange ideas and resources. In addition, by sharing the feel-good stories associated with your mementos you are not only rehearsing your good feelings and alternative story in front of an audience but you are also honouring all the special people in your life that are represented in the photos and mementos in that treasure chest.**

The treasure chest can also be thought of as a metaphor for all the things you hold close to your heart. Often when we feel strong emotions such as love, caring, loyalty and commitment we feel them in our chest, close to where our heart is. These emotions are usually associated with the people we are closest to. Similarly, we can often feel painful emotions in our chest too, such as hurt, betrayal, regret and sorrow. Funnily enough, these emotions too are usually associated with the people we are closest to. It is our loved ones who fill our chests with precious gems like funny moments, loving words, warm smiles and soft, gentle hugs.

Sometimes loved ones make withdrawals on the treasures in your chest by using harsh words, hurting your feelings or taking you for granted. The important point to remember is that as long as you are spending enough time and effort with your loved ones to fill up each other's treasure chests you don't have to worry about a few withdrawals now and then. It is only when we are not giving each other enough treasured moments that we have to worry about the withdrawal rate depleting our abundance and eventually making our relationship bankrupt. It is important to keep to the forefront of your mind that all the golden moments you spend with your loved ones enrich both your life and theirs. Be generous with your time and practise loving-kindness towards your loved ones as often as possible.

Many people we have worked with have found the following poem useful as a way of keeping their loving-kindness project to the forefront of their mind.

THE LOVING-KINDNESS POEM EXERCISE
May I be filled with loving-kindness
May I be well
May I be peaceful and at ease
May I be happy.

You can recite this poem to yourself at the end of any of the relaxation and meditation exercises we have outlined in this book.

This chapter has touched on some of the important aspects of nurturing your relationship with yourself, your significant others and stress and anxiety. Feelings about our relationships can often change like the weather. Some days relationships are cloudy, dark and threatening and it can feel as if it is the end of the world. But just remember: this, too, shall pass. Similarly, some days your relationships are clear, fine and sunny and life is just perfect. Just remember: this, too, shall pass. Again, the point is that feelings do not provide the most stable foundations for relationships. Alternatively, we tend to have a bit more control over our behaviours and with some effort we can work to make our actions more constant and reliable. We can then act in ways that help us travel towards relationships that are more accepting, compassionate and kind.

TRAVEL REMINDERS

Here are some reminders from this chapter. You may want to copy them and make them into a reminder card to place in your diary or wallet, or even on the fridge or a mirror at home.

- Our relationship with stress and anxiety is similar to other relationships – sometimes it feels as though the stress/anxiety is trying to wreak havoc on your life.
- Acceptance involves recognising the way things are and is the first step towards change.
- Learning to sit with feelings and avoiding avoidance is a pathway to acceptance.
- Values are about the journey, while goals are about the destination.
- Self-acceptance means accepting yourself as a valuable human being and being all right with who you are.
- Self-compassion means that you are kind and understanding of yourself.

TRAVEL DIARY

BRINGING IT
ALL TOGETHER

> What lies behind us and what lies
> before us are tiny matters compared
> to what lies within us.

> —Ralph Waldo Emerson (1803–82)

In Chapter 1 we spoke about the term 'disorder'. We said that when anxiety symptoms are distressing and interfere with the person's ability to carry out their daily activities, the degree of anxiety is significant and is referred to as an anxiety disorder. We also spoke of a number of anxiety disorders, namely generalised anxiety disorder (GAD), panic disorder (PD), agoraphobia, specific phobias, social anxiety disorder (SAD), health anxiety, obsessive-compulsive disorder (OCD) and adjustment disorder and post-traumatic stress disorder (PTSD). Refer back to Chapter 1, in which we introduced each of these. We will also discuss health anxiety, as although this is not formally considered to be an anxiety disorder, it is a common and distressing problem in practice and, as the title suggests, is viewed as anxiety about health.[1]

We are torn about using labels such as these, as our experience is that labels are beneficial in some ways but not in others. It can be helpful to understand the nature of the particular anxiety symptoms as these will guide treatment, and to have a common language to talk about the issues. However, as we suggested in Chapter 3, it is tempting to buy into the label of the 'disorder', thinking and behaving like someone with an anxiety disorder and coming to believe that you are the anxiety disorder. When reading this chapter, remember that the anxiety is the problem and it is separate it from you, the person.

We also outlined that our approach to managing anxiety is multimodal, or in other words, choosing strategies or skills from several different therapy models, depending on the issues of the individual. In this book we have drawn on a range of therapies, including:

- Motivational Interviewing
- Cognitive Behavioural Therapy
- Narrative Therapy
- Relaxation Therapy
- Hypnotherapy
- Mindfulness
- Constructive Living
- Acceptance and Commitment Therapy.

You will have seen that each of these therapies is valuable in managing anxiety, and each has a range of useful practical strategies. In this chapter we will summarise and add to the key strategies from these different psychological approaches that are useful for particular anxiety disorders.

Remember that thorough assessment, including a general check-up, is part of early management to exclude any physical causes of the symptoms or co-existing problems such as depression. Medication may be necessary if the symptoms are severe, and is best used in combination with psychological treatments.

Different travels mean different plans!

We will now revisit the specific types of anxiety disorders, and the treatment approaches and strategies which may assist. You will notice that there are some commonalities between which approaches can help each type of disorder, but also specific strategies for specific disorders. This section is a summary. A therapist can provide more information and advice about how to put the different techniques into practice, and there are also some excellent resources available (these are highlighted in the 'Further Resources' section at the end of the book).

Generalised anxiety disorder

In GAD, the individual experiences excessive and persistent worry about a variety of general life issues, such as work or family. Often the person says that they 'have always been a worrier', and it may seem as if they worry all the time, about any issue, no matter how small. People who experience GAD are pushed around by the belief that they can do little to predict and control events in life, so they end up worrying about them. However, worrying can be unproductive as it often stops people engaging in activity and in problem-solving the issues.[2]

Below are some useful treatment approaches and strategies.

- Psycho-education or the provision of information on the nature of stress and anxiety and common myths. See Chapter 1.
- Set some goals by considering the different domains in life and your values. See Chapter 2.
- Reduce your stress bucket via relaxation techniques, including breathing techniques, progressive muscle relaxation or visualisation techniques. Consider yoga or tai chi. See chapters 2 and 3.
- Get back to balance, including a healthy lifestyle, good nutrition, regular exercise and sleep hygiene. Remember to reduce caffeine or intake of other stimulating drugs. See Chapter 3. Also return to activities (whether work, social or leisure) that are meaningful to you.
- Use mindfulness techniques. These can be helpful for relaxation, and also to ground you in the moment instead of worrying about the future or the past. See chapters 3 and 4.
- Utilise CBT – identify unhelpful tricks and traps in your thinking (via awareness and thought diaries) and use strategies to deal with them, such as looking for other perspectives, checking for evidence and using different words. Consider core beliefs and use the downward arrow technique. See Chapter 4.
- Surf your anxious feelings: be aware of them, observe them, catch them early, stay just ahead of them by using your relaxation or cognitive techniques. Notice that the wave finishes and anxiety does not go on and on forever. See Chapter 4.
- Take action: for example, use problem-solving or assertiveness strategies if appropriate. See Chapter 5.
- Utilise ACT principles, including contact with the present moment (or mindfulness), defusion (for example, 'I am

having the thought that . . . '), acceptance (of uncomfortable feelings), self-as-context, values and committed action (practise relaxation and other techniques). See Chapter 6 for a range of ACT strategies which may assist.

- Write down the thoughts to relieve anxiety, and to also help you step back from the thoughts.

- Utilise narrative principles such as externalising the anxiety, considering how the anxiety has impacted on your life, and how you have been able to take a stand against the anxiety. What qualities in you helped you do this, and how can they help you now? Reconnect with important people in your life who see you as separate from the problem. See Chapter 7.

- Use Hypnotherapy – for general relaxation and specific suggestions to reduce anxiety and build self-confidence. Consider seeing a qualified hypnotherapist or using relaxation/hypnotherapy CDs, such as our CD for stress and anxiety.

- Be kind and compassionate to yourself. See Chapter 8.

Panic disorder

In PD an individual has recurring and unanticipated periods of intense fear, which are followed by persistent concern about having further attacks.

Below are some useful treatment approaches and strategies.

- Get information on the nature of stress and panic episodes. Individuals may misinterpret the symptoms as being serious, so it is important to understand the bodily changes involved in the fight or flight response. See Chapter 1. Also, consider educating key family members or friends so that they can provide support.

- Get reassurance that the bodily symptoms are not serious, and debunk some of the myths about anxiety, such as 'you are losing control or going crazy', 'you're going to faint or have a heart attack'. See Chapter 1.
- Engage in goal setting. See Chapter 2.
- Think about what strategies you have used in the past and which ones were most helpful. Try them again.
- Recognise hyperventilation or rapid breathing. Time your breathing as we described in Chapter 3. Then try diaphragmatic or abdominal breathing. In panic, a particular abdominal breathing technique called 'slow breathing' is used, producing a breathing rate of around 10 breaths per minute.[3] This technique is central for managing panic and should be practised on a daily basis.

SLOW BREATHING TECHNIQUE EXERCISE

Stop what you are doing, sit down if you can and breathe in and out slowly. Take medium breaths (not deep or shallow breaths), breathing down to your abdomen. Breathe in a 6-second cycle, that is, breathe in to the count of three, and then out for the count of three: in, two, three; out, two, three.

- Utilise other relaxation techniques, such as muscle relaxation or visualisation. See chapters 2 and 3.
- Get back to balance and activities that are meaningful to you. Consider yoga or tai chi. See Chapter 3.
- Use mindfulness techniques. See Chapter 3.
- Use CBT, aiming to identify unhelpful thoughts associated with panic and challenging them ('I am not going crazy or losing control . . . '), putting them in perspective ('What would it matter if I vomited; if I

passed out someone would help me and I would recover
. . .'), or letting them go. See Chapter 5.
- Have a card with more helpful thoughts written on it and
carry it in your bag. It might list some things that are
helpful when you feel panicky, such as to breathe and
relax, or to say, 'I'm okay, the feelings will pass'. An
example is given in Figure 8.

FIGURE 8: OVERCOMING PANIC CARD
- It is just panic, simply breathe and relax.
- Breathe in, two, three and out, two, three. Breathe in
peace and calm, breathe out and relax.
- I'm okay, the feelings will pass.
- I have had these feelings before, and I know that I
am safe.
- Have a glass of water or count backwards from
twenty.

- Surf your panicky feelings: be aware of them, observe
them, catch them early, stay just ahead of them by using
your relaxation or cognitive techniques. And notice that
the wave finishes as anxiety does not go on and on
forever. See Chapter 4.
- A technique to manage the panic cascade (described in
Chapter 4): identify the initial symptoms of panic, and the
associated thoughts and feelings. Read the example given in
Table 10 overleaf and use the spare rows for yourself. What
are the early symptoms and is there an underlying fear?
Intervene early with slow breathing, and helpful thoughts
(you might use your card with helpful thoughts written
on it).[4]

TABLE 10: DEALING WITH THE PANIC CASCADE

Symptom	Thought	Feeling
Heart racing	Oh no, I am going to have a panic attack	Frightened
Chest pain	It's getting worse	Anxious
Breathing fast	I am going to have a heart attack	Terrified

- Utilise ACT principles, including contact with the present moment (or mindfulness), defusion (for example, 'I am having the thought that . . . '), acceptance (of uncomfortable feelings), self-as-context, values and committed action (practise relaxation and other techniques). See Chapter 6 for a range of ACT strategies which may assist.
- Utilise narrative principles such as externalising the panic, considering how the panic has impacted on your life, and how you have been able to take a stand against the panic. What qualities in you helped you do this, and how can they help you now? Reconnect with important people in your life who see you as separate from the problem. Refer to Chapter 7.
- Use Hypnotherapy – for general relaxation and specific suggestions to reduce anxiety and build self-confidence. Consider seeing a qualified hypnotherapist or using relaxation/hypnotherapy CDs, such as our CD for stress and anxiety.
- Be kind and compassionate to yourself. See Chapter 8.

Agoraphobia

Agoraphobia may be associated with panic disorder. With agoraphobia, the individual is anxious about being in a situation in which it may be difficult to escape or which may be embarrassing. They may be anxious about being able to find help if they do something humiliating or show obvious anxiety symptoms. This anxiety usually leads to avoidance of the feared situations, such as crowded places, buses or shopping centres. Consider Craig's story.

CRAIG'S STORY

Craig lives near a large shopping complex. He never liked going there, as it has a long mall, with the only exits being at each end. As he moved along the mall, he would become very panicky. One weekend he had a severe panic attack and fled the centre. From that time he became fearful of having panic attacks at the shops and he would avoid them. A month later, on his way to work he again had a severe panic attack. He turned back home. The panic attacks became more frequent and Craig found that he was reluctant to leave the house. He has not been out for six weeks, and is fearful of losing his job.

All of the strategies for panic attacks mentioned on pages 232–235 will assist Craig, including psycho-education, breathing and relaxation techniques and cognitive strategies. He also needs to consider a graded exposure program, such as the one designed for John in Chapter 5. In graded exposure a list of steps to gradually tackle anxiety-provoking situations is worked out. The steps are ranked from least anxiety-provoking to most anxiety-provoking. A therapist would then work with Craig to progress through the steps, with the least difficult scenario tackled first, followed by the next difficult and then the next. Each step is carried out until it causes less anxiety (at least 50 per cent less) and then Craig will move on to the next. Ultimately Craig will be able to go about his shopping and work and other daily activities.

Specific phobia

With specific phobias, an individual has an unrelenting and irrational fear of a specific object or situation, such as fear of enclosed spaces (claustrophobia), or a fear related to an animal or heights. This fear usually leads to avoidance of the object or situation. Below are some useful treatment approaches and strategies.

- Get information on the nature of the phobia.
- Engage in goal setting. See Chapter 2.
- Gain some reassurance that the bodily symptoms are not serious. See Chapter 2.
- Utilise abdominal breathing techniques and relaxation techniques. See Chapter 3.
- Use graded exposure, as discussed above. Also, refer back to the example of John in Chapter 5.
- Be kind and compassionate to yourself. See Chapter 8.
- Use Hypnotherapy – imaginal exposure techniques may assist, that is, graded exposure can in part be carried out in the imagination. An example is imagining a picture of a spider in a book, or imagining spraying the spider with insect spray.

Social anxiety disorder

In SAD, the individual is anxious about being negatively appraised by others, in case they do something embarrassing or show obvious anxiety symptoms. This anxiety usually leads to avoidance of the feared situations, such as eating, speaking in front of others, or going to social gatherings.

Below are some useful treatment approaches and strategies.

- Get information on the nature of social anxiety.
- Engage in goal setting. Base your goals on your values. What do you want to achieve and why? See Chapter 2.
- Gain some reassurance that the bodily symptoms are not serious, and debunk some of the myths about anxiety. See Chapter 2.
- Think about what strategies you have used in the past and which ones were most helpful. Try them again.
- Utilise abdominal breathing and relaxation techniques. See Chapter 3.
- Get back to balance and activities that are meaningful to you. Refer to Chapter 3.
- Use mindfulness techniques to focus on the moment and not worry about the 'what ifs'. See Chapter 3.
- Utilise CBT, aiming to identify unhelpful thoughts associated with the social anxiety and challenging them ('I am not an idiot, people are not looking at me . . . ') or putting them into perspective ('What would it matter if I said the wrong thing? In fact, most people are thinking about themselves and not me.'). Consider underlying beliefs that may be driving these thoughts, such as 'I must be approved of by everyone, I have to be competent', and challenge them or let them go.[5] See Chapter 4.

- Have a card with more helpful thoughts written on it and carry it in your bag. It might list some things that are helpful such as to breathe and relax, or to say: 'I'm okay, the feelings will pass.' (See page 239.)
- Surf panicky feelings associated with social anxiety: be aware of them, observe them, catch them early, stay just ahead of them by using your relaxation or cognitive techniques. See Chapter 4.
- Learn social skills, including assertiveness (covered in Chapter 5). Remember too that individuals are quite focused on themselves. A great way to engage them is to ask questions about their lives. This also takes the focus off you until you feel more comfortable.
- Sometimes in therapy you and the therapist may decide that taking a video of you talking to others would be helpful. The video would be played back to you to reassure you that you look fine and that people cannot see that you are experiencing anxiety.
- Develop a graded programme for engaging in social activities, beginning with the least challenging occasions; for example, an individual might begin with a social occasion with one or two close friends at a friend's house, and later move towards a work dinner. Refer to Chapter 5.
- Utilise ACT principles, including contact with the present moment (or mindfulness), defusion (for example, 'I am having the thought that . . . '), acceptance (of uncomfortable feelings), self-as-context (observe the thoughts and be non-judgemental), values and committed action (practise relaxation and other techniques). See Chapter 6 for a range of ACT strategies which may assist, including 'unpacking the acceptance of emotions'.
- Utilise narrative principles such as externalising the anxiety, considering how it has impacted on your life, and

how you have been able to take a stand against it. What qualities in you helped you do this, and how can they help you now? Reconnect with important people in your life who see you as separate from the problem. See Chapter 7.

• Use Hypnotherapy – for general relaxation and specific suggestions to reduce anxiety, techniques such as mental rehearsal of social situations or rehearsal in the imagination, and techniques to build self-confidence. Consider seeing a qualified hypnotherapist or using relaxation/hypnotherapy CDs, such as our CD for stress and anxiety.

• Be kind and compassionate to yourself. See Chapter 8.

Obsessive-compulsive disorder

In OCD the individual may experience unpleasant, intrusive obsessional thoughts, ideas, images, and impulses that they find difficult to control, such as concerns about contaminating or harming themselves or their family. These obsessional thoughts often lead to repetitive behaviours, including hand-washing or checking. These behaviours are performed on the basis of preventing the occurrence of the unlikely event (such as harm to children), or to reduce anxiety; that is, the ritual has the effect of reducing discomfort.

We suggest that individuals with OCD work with a therapist to guide them through the most appropriate treatment strategies. However, helpful strategies in OCD include those listed below.

• Get information on the nature of OCD and in particular the obsessions and compulsions.

• Engage in goal-setting. See Chapter 2.

- Gain some reassurance that the bodily symptoms are not serious, and debunk some of the myths about anxiety.
- Think about what strategies you have used in the past and which ones were most helpful. Try them again.
- Use breathing and relaxation techniques. See Chapter 3.
- Use mindfulness techniques. See Chapter 3.
- Get back to balance and activities that are meaningful to you. Refer to Chapter 3.
- Use CBT, aiming to identify unhelpful thoughts associated with OCD and challenging them ('Unless I check, some harm will come to my family'), or letting them go.
- Graded exposure techniques have been shown to be effective in OCD. The therapist will assist the individual in identifying triggers that cause discomfort, such as having an untidy kitchen or empty cupboards, or different work situations. Internal cues are also identified, that is, thoughts ('Did I leave the oven on?'), feelings or images. The individual then rates the triggers in relation to how anxiety-provoking they are, and rituals and the situations which are avoided are also identified. A programme is then developed to help the individual carry out exposure to different tasks and limits are placed on ritualised behaviours.[6] It is important to remember that these techniques are carried out in small steps, and progress is gradual. See Chapter 5.
- Utilise ACT principles, including contact with the present moment (or mindfulness), defusion (for example, 'I am having the thought that . . . '), acceptance (of uncomfortable feelings), self-as-context, values and committed action (practise relaxation and other techniques). See Chapter 6 for a range of ACT strategies which may assist.

- Utilise narrative principles such as externalising the obsessions and compulsions, considering how the OCD has impacted on your life, and how you have been able to take a stand against it. What qualities in you helped you do this, and how can they help you now? Reconnect with important people in your life who see you as separate from the problem. Refer to Chapter 7.
- Use Hypnotherapy – for general relaxation and specific suggestions to reduce anxiety and build self-confidence. Imaginal exposure techniques may assist. Consider seeing a qualified hypnotherapist or using relaxation/hypnotherapy CDs, such as our CD for stress and anxiety.
- Be kind and compassionate to yourself. See Chapter 8.

Adjustment disorder and post-traumatic stress disorder

Adjustment disorder and PTSD are seen as reactions to severe stress. They operate on a continuum, with a mild reaction to stress at one end, adjustment disorders in the middle, and PTSD at the severe end of the spectrum.[7]

Adjustment disorder involves severe anxiety in response to an acute illness or psychological stress (such as a relationship breakdown). Emotional or behavioural symptoms of distress may arise and interfere with functioning but not last more than six months.[8] Treatment of adjustment disorder may include psycho-education, support, relaxation strategies, CBT, ACT, Narrative Therapy and Hypnotherapy.

PTSD involves the development of long-lasting anxiety following a traumatic event (such as an accident or rape). It is characterised by images, dreams or flashbacks of the event and a range of other symptoms.[9] Treatment of PTSD is more complex than other anxiety disorders and it is important that you seek guidance from an experienced therapist. Treatment approaches that are used include psycho-education, support, stress management, medication, CBT (including systematic imaginal exposure), Hypnotherapy and ACT.

Another therapy that may be utilised is Eye Movement Desensitisation Reprocessing (EMDR). EMDR is based on the idea that during a traumatic event, information about the experience can be stored in the mind in an unprocessed way. In EMDR the person is asked to focus on the event whilst moving their eyes in certain ways, to assist in processing the information.[10]

Health anxiety

Health anxiety refers to experiencing excessive worry and concern about one's health, to the point where symptoms are troublesome or daily functioning is interfered with. There may be concern about having a serious illness, for example.

Management may involve a health check at the outset, reassurance and information. CBT can be helpful in assisting the person to identify the thoughts provoking anxiety, and to challenge them. Relaxation, mindfulness and ACT approaches may also assist. Learning to not focus on the 'what ifs' of the future are important, and strategies to sit with the anxiety can assist.

It is often useful to have an ongoing relationship with one GP so that they are aware of your concerns. This also avoids unnecessary tests and procedures. The individual with health anxiety may feel the need to attend a doctor's surgery frequently, to check each new symptom. One approach in dealing with this is to have regular but less frequent appointments, such as every six weeks, to monitor progress.

So your travel kit is filling up

This chapter has summarised some of the key approaches and strategies that may be useful with particular anxiety problems. The aim is to fill up your travel kit so that you have a number of options. You know yourself well and you know what has been tried before, and so you can work out which of these ideas might be useful for you to now try. Some of the strategies will require help from a therapist, and some you can try yourself. If you are not sure, then talk about them with your GP or therapist. Remember too that it is worth trying some things again, or trying things which might not sound like they would suit you – you may be surprised.

Caring for carers

This section is for family, friends, support people or carers. We hope that you have found this book useful in understanding stress and anxiety. The more that you understand about these issues, the more you can empathise with the individual experiencing stress and anxiety. Sometimes too, you will be the person guiding them to perhaps access some professional help, or to think about getting back to their relaxation or other stress management strategies. You might be able to assist them with some of the ideas we have presented in the book.

Also, being a friend or carer can be stressful. So it is important to apply many of the self-care ideas to yourself and to prevent your stress bucket from building up too much or overflowing. It is important for you to consider balance in your own life, and perhaps do the 'Eggs in a basket' exercise in Chapter 3. Sometimes the pressures of caring can lead to anxiety or depression in the carer, and so remember to seek early help if you are concerned about this. There are also carer organisations or other non-government organisations focusing on anxiety which can assist.

TRAVEL REMINDERS

Here are some reminders from this chapter. You may want to copy them and make them into a reminder card to place in your diary or wallet, or even on the fridge or a mirror at home.

- **There is a range of approaches and strategies for managing each anxiety disorder.**
- **A thorough assessment and general check-up are important at the outset.**
- **Management generally involves provision of information and goal setting based on your values.**
- **Relaxation and breathing techniques are central, as well as getting back to balance and meaningful activities.**
- **Mindfulness and CBT techniques are generally part of management.**
- **ACT or Narrative Therapy principles may assist.**
- **Be kind and compassionate to yourself.**
- **Hypnotherapy may be appropriate.**
- **Treatment for OCD and PTSD in particular require specialist knowledge and guidance from an experienced therapist.**

TRAVEL DIARY

THE END OF THIS JOURNEY, BUT NOT THE END OF THE STORY

The world is a book and those who do not travel read only one page.

—St Augustine (354–430AD)

We have almost reached the end of this book, which has aimed to help you on your journey by providing you with knowledge, ideas and skills to bring about change. In this chapter we will review some of the key ideas from the book which, as we have written them or taught them in the past, have really resonated with us and our clients or students. We think the reason they stand out to us is that they are simple, useful and practical ideas that people can really relate to.

But first, what are some of these ideas or approaches that have resonated with you?

_____

_____

_____

_____

_____

_____

We will also encourage you to celebrate your progress or victories in recovery from stress and anxiety. Remember that even partial success is a success.

Review of key ideas

We have used the journey metaphor throughout this book, as it fits with life and managing challenges which arise along the way, such as stress and anxiety. We are designed to respond to stress. Anxiety is a universal human emotion, and it is a lot like fear. We talked about the fight or flight response which explains the various physical symptoms of stress or anxiety. Stress can be helpful at times, but when it is excessive or chronic, difficulties can arise.

Courage and hope can assist us in our journey with stress and anxiety. You have shown courage in reading this book and trying some of the techniques within it. We reiterate now that there is hope in this journey, and resources such as this and perhaps working with a therapist can assist you to find this hope. One of the most important messages in this book is to always take things one small step at a time. This will help you to feel secure in your journey, to make progress and to see each small success along the way.

During this journey, we have invited you to use your expert knowledge about yourself to make choices about which ideas or strategies suit you. It is also vital that you apply compassion to yourself along the way, just as you do to others. This includes looking after yourself – your nutrition, fitness and rest. This is part of a holistic approach to managing stress and anxiety.

At the beginning of your journey we suggested that you make some travel plans, and we asked you to consider what you value in the different domains in life, and which domains you might focus on. For example, you might have chosen health, relationships, leisure or work, and these choices will have shaped your own personal goals. We suggest that you go back to Table 5 (page 49) when you have a moment, and review whether the gaps you identified earlier still exist or not. This is a good way of marking your progress. We also suggest that you revisit goal setting as outlined in Chapter 2 from time to time.

During this journey we have identified potential blocks in the road, such as 'instant gratification' or wanting a quick fix. We live in a fast world, with technology everywhere, and as a result we are all used to quick results. However, the sort of approaches that we have presented take practice and often time to take effect. We encourage you to stick with the strategies that you think are most helpful for you, and keep practising. We have mentioned in several places in the book that the human brain can change, and part of the potential for change involves effort.

Throughout this book we have drawn upon a number of therapies that have great merit. The approach of choosing particular therapies which will be best for a particular individual, and combining them, is called multimodal. This is our preferred way of working, and this approach is well received by clients and professionals. Treatment of stress or anxiety may also involve medication or complementary therapies, and your GP or therapist can advise you further on these.

The stress bucket idea was introduced in Chapter 3. We have seen individuals or couples react with delight and amazement to this simple concept. How did it fit for you? All of us can work on reducing the level of stress in our bucket, and one of the key means of doing this is relaxation. Relaxation is the body's way of dealing with stress, and there are many techniques which can help you calm the breath, the body and the mind. Return to Chapter 3 and revisit the different relaxation strategies regularly. We addressed some of the common barriers to using these techniques in that chapter and again these are worth revisiting and eliminating from our daily lives.

We all crave balance in our lives. This can refer to the right amount of relaxation and stress in life, but also balance between the different domains in life.

Remember the eggs in the basket exercise in Chapter 3. How are your baskets right now?

_____

_____

_____

_____

_____

_____

What can you do this week to redress any imbalances, and how can you take better care of yourself generally?

_____

_____

_____

_____

_____

_____

In Chapter 4, we discussed some of the common myths about anxiety, and suggested that labelling is not always helpful, and that happiness is not a constant state of mind. This chapter focused on CBT and we hope that the exercises made this therapy real for you. It is one of the most helpful approaches that we utilise, both for ourselves and our clients. Again, change with CBT takes time and effort, but the effort is worthwhile. Have you found that being aware of unhelpful thinking styles (such as black and white thinking, or catastrophising) has been helpful? What about the techniques for challenging unhelpful thoughts (such as checking out evidence or reframing thoughts)? We encourage you to experiment with these and see which ones work best for you.

The concept of mindfulness has been talked about in several chapters. This is an essential item in your travel kit! If we can focus on the present moment more, and in a non-judgemental way, we will see improvement. Worrying about the future does not exist when we are mindful, and we feel more calm and relaxed. We can also be mindfully aware of our thoughts, observing them and choosing whether or not to let them pass. This is the essence of MBCT.

With fear, behaviours which lead to avoidance (such as escape) are common. The behavioural strategies involved in CBT involve avoiding avoidance! The thought of graded exposure can be challenging, but when carried out in a step-by-step way, and assisted by breathing and thinking techniques, can be very achievable and successful. A therapist can assist with such techniques. We also looked at procrastination, which is another way of avoiding and often a problem for individuals who set high standards for themselves, but again the strategies to deal with this are very useful. Revisit them from time to time, and also problem-solving or assertiveness as these can be extremely helpful in your travel kit.

Chapter 6 focused on ACT, a relatively new behavioural therapy, which assists us to develop more psychological flexibility and to take action to create a rich and meaningful life. It incorporates six key processes, including mindfulness, defusion from anxiety-related thoughts, acceptance of things that cannot be controlled in life, getting in touch with our observing mind and taking committed action based on our values. ACT suggests that struggling with anxiety-provoking thoughts and feelings is a problem, and teaches us how to sit with our feelings at the same time as developing more comfort in ourselves.

One of the ideas we emphasised from ACT and Constructive Living is taking action. A powerful way of thinking about this is to think about how we want people to view us when we are gone. Do we want them to say that we had wanted to do certain things (like volunteer for a charity), that we wished that we had, or that we actually had? We are remembered for our actions. The old saying 'Actions speak louder than words' is a good reminder to focus on action in life.

In Chapter 7 we explored some of the ideas central to Narrative Therapy. We learnt that adversity does not necessarily build character, but reveals it. One of the assumptions of Narrative Therapy is that stress and anxiety disconnects us from our own resources. You have probably already rediscovered many skills, abilities, qualities and values that you have used in the past to deal with stress and anxiety. One of the most reassuring aspects of reading a book like this is to recognise that you already had a lot of the knowledge the book has covered. Narrative Therapy makes clear that stress and anxiety are the problem and you are not the problem.

We also addressed the notion that problems such as stress and anxiety are manufactured in a social, cultural and political context. For example, it is not safe to attempt to reduce someone's stress and anxiety if they are in an abusive relationship. The problem here is abuse, not stress and anxiety. Finally, the other main idea in this chapter was about choice. You can choose to labour under a dominant story that is impoverishing your life and that privileges stress and anxiety as the main characters. Or you can work to live your preferred story that is enriching of your life. The journey provided by Narrative Therapy has no right way, just many possible directions. These directions are chosen by you. The path you choose represents the alternative story to the stress/anxiety story. It is not just any path or any alternative story; it is the story by which you would choose to live your life.

Chapter 8 explored the importance of acceptance, compassion and kindness. It was not able to address the complex area of relationships in depth, but looked at some aspects. We learnt that acceptance is a vital step before making changes and involves a readiness to recognise how things are. We defined self-esteem and discussed some of the problems associated with this construct. Then we offered an alternative to self-esteem in the form of self-acceptance and self-compassion, and highlighted the benefits of being kind to ourselves and others. We also outlined some practical exercises and steps you can take to incorporate acceptance, compassion and kindness into your relationships and your life.

More travel stories: ideas for celebrations

When people have been on an overseas trip they often like to share stories, photos and mementos of their journey, and they usually share these with the important people in their life when they return home. This may serve several important purposes.

Firstly, by telling their stories and showing their photos they are able to relive the good feelings they had during that travel experience. As we said in Chapter 8, memories are encoded with feeling states.

When someone tells their story they perform a type of mental rehearsal that helps them memorise the details of that story. It follows that the more frequent the retelling of the story the less easy it will be to forget the details of that trip.

Gaining an audience to the telling and retelling of the story makes the story more real. Friends and family like to ask questions about your trip that can trigger forgotten aspects and help you enjoy them again.

Telling travel stories provides people with an opportunity to catch up on how you have changed because of the journey. In a sense, people get to meet the new you.

You have been on a journey too, the one to let go of stress and anxiety. As such you may like to celebrate your journey on your own, perhaps by making a list of your progress or victories on this journey – no matter how small. You might like to use the 'Travel diary' page at the end of this chapter, and on that list might be things such as:

- I learnt more about stress and anxiety by reading this book.
- I thought about what I value in my life, and set some goals for myself.
- I realised that I have a lot of 'eggs in a (couple of) basket(s)' and need to find more balance.
- I am working on being more mindful, especially when I go for a walk.
- I am more aware of thoughts that trigger feelings of anxiety, and I am learning to let them go.
- I am being kinder to myself.

It is also useful to notice at what stage in this journey you noticed change, or whether there were any particular turning points for you. For example, one client reported that when they took on board the idea that thoughts are only thoughts and not facts, this was a turning point for them. Another said that realising they needed to show themselves the same kindness they show others was their turning point.

Have you noticed any turning points in your journey?

_____

_____

_____

_____

_____

_____

_____

You might also share your travel story with the important people in your life. Sometimes celebrations and rituals are used to mark progress or change in our society. You might like to use a celebration or ritual to mark and celebrate your journey away from stress and anxiety towards a new and preferred version of life. Celebrations and rituals to mark your progress can be anything you choose. They can be formal or informal, they can be held at any venue that is meaningful to you and they can include cakes, balloons, speeches, slide shows and before-and-after snapshots. The ritual or celebration will benefit from being structured in a way that most powerfully acknowledges all that has been experienced on your journey.[1]

Relapse prevention

Now that you have reached the last chapter in this book and learnt new knowledge, behaviours and skills, it is important to think about how you will keep on learning and how you will maintain the new ideas and ways of being. It can be helpful to ask yourself the following questions:

What skills have I found most useful?

_____

_____

_____

_____

_____

_____

_____

What things might get in the way of my new ideas, behaviours or skills?

How can I deal with these situations?[2,3]

_____

_____

_____

_____

_____

_____

It is important to look after your general health, such as nutrition, sleep and exercise. If medication is part of the management, it is important to keep using it while prescribed. Stay in touch with your GP or therapist in relation to this. It is useful to touch base from time to time with your GP or therapist about your progress. They will get to know you over time and will be a useful resource and support, but will also notice how you are travelling and give you feedback. They can also help you to develop a plan for managing relapse (or a return of symptoms) if it was to occur.[4]

Such a plan involves three steps, namely:

- Identifying early warning symptoms, such as sleep disturbance or irritability.
- Identifying possible high-risk situations for relapse. Ask yourself, what are my stressors and which ones create stress or anxiety; for example, job pressures, ill-health, family upset. Also consider what you might do to protect yourself if these issues arise.

- Preparing an emergency plan to put into action if you suspect a relapse. The plan might involve talking with friends or family, being mindful, using relaxation techniques, revisiting earlier chapters in this book, seeing your GP or therapist.[5,6]

RELAPSE PREVENTION PLAN EXERCISE
After considering what elements would be helpful to you as an individual, you might like to write a draft of your relapse prevention plan on the 'Travel diary' page so it is there if needed in the future.

Final words

To let go of stress and anxiety and get the life you want you may need to experience some difficulty. Stress and anxiety are not your enemies, they are your teachers. We can only know things by knowing their opposites. We know light by knowing dark, we know courage by knowing fear and we know happiness by knowing sadness. Unfortunately, you cannot fully appreciate one without the other. However, moments of adversity and pain provide you with opportunities for growth and change. They teach you important skills and help give you perspective on life.[7]

In Constructive Living there is a view that suffering always comes from the distortion of some positive source, known as the beautiful source or the kernel of good. For example, phobias about cancer come from the desire to be healthy, social phobia comes from the desire to be respected and liked, perfectionism comes from the desire to do well, and so on. Knowing that there is a beautiful source may not make the suffering less painful but it offers a clue about how to address the issue. The suffering directs you towards useful and important information. You don't need to be in love with your suffering but you can invite it to be your teacher.[8]

We found these ideas particularly useful in helping us to write this book, and we would like to share our story of our journey in writing this book with you now.

CATE AND MICHELE'S STORY

Writing this last chapter encouraged us to reflect on what the journey of writing this book has been like for us. You may be surprised to know that we may have been taking a parallel journey to you. We started this journey with our dream that we could make some people's lives better. This dream was driven by a strong value of caring for people and our wish to make a difference. We started this journey full of hope, energy and clarity about our direction and purpose.

The first chapters were powered by great enthusiasm and focus and we believed we were right on track. Then other life demands interrupted our flow and focus and for a while we lost our way. At this time we were vulnerable to stress, anxiety, self-doubt and other unhelpful characters. Anxiety took the opportunity to tell us, 'What if you don't finish the book on time? What if people find it boring, unhelpful, hard to understand and wrong? What if people criticise your ideas and writing style? What makes your book any better than the hundreds of stress and anxiety books already on the shelves?'

Our judgemental thinking minds told us all sorts of interesting stories such as: 'This book is not good

---

enough, it has to be perfect and if it is not perfect people will think you are stupid and lazy.' Suffice to say there were a few times when we felt our journey had entered a dark tunnel and there did not seem to be a light at the end of it. There was also a fair bit of procrastination, catastrophising, unhelpful thinking and not much doing going on. The stress and anxiety were very good at disconnecting us from our own strengths, abilities, skills, knowledge and values. At the times we felt we had lost sight of our direction, we turned back to our values and our original reason for writing this book to gain inspiration to keep going, one small step at a time. We got reconnected with what drives us. We also started to do what we had written about in the book. To our immense relief it actually works!

At other times our journey had great highs, as almost everyone we told about the book said, 'I could use a copy of that when it is finished.' Also many clients, friends and relatives offered us so much wonderful support in so many different ways. This provided us with hope at the times when we worried that our parents would be the only people to purchase a copy of our book. We also had a back-up plan of giving copies to friends and relatives as birthday and Christmas presents!

At times our journey was reminiscent of the start of a family holiday which would involve a four-day driving trip – you know the ones where you would just get out of the driveway and your three-year-old asks, 'Are we there yet?' Many times Cate and I pondered 'Are we there yet?' Again we had to remind ourselves not to be pushed around by a 'sense of urgency' and just to keep taking small, consistent steps towards our goal of writing this book. We worked to accept that our project was ambitious and there were no easy ways or shortcuts to writing the book. There was also the sneaky thought that tricked us into wanting to know that things would all turn out right in the end: 'If we just knew that the book would help people then all of this hard work and discomfort would be worth it.'

Then we would remind ourselves that life is not like that; life is about the journey or the process and not the destination. Instead we remembered to focus on how we were taking a risk to do something that we valued and believed in. And regardless of the outcome, the opportunity to write this book and to learn was too big to avoid just because we might feel some uncomfortable or painful feelings along the way.

Finally, all along this road we tried to be kind and compassionate to ourselves and to keep at the forefront of our mind that imperfection, stress and anxiety are all part of the human condition. Reminding ourselves of our own humanness was very reassuring as it stopped us feeling alone on this journey. It also allowed us to reconnect with our own knowledge of hope, patience and effort. The fuel that powered our drive to write this book for you was the hope and belief that the ideas written in this book can help make things better for people experiencing stress and anxiety.

You can see from our story that we found ourselves reflecting on and using some of the key messages in the book while writing it. We found that we needed to focus on the importance of values, taking small steps, being mindful and taking action, as well as being kind and compassionate towards ourselves. Notice too how we reflected on life being about the journey and not the destination. If you think about a train trip between major cities, if you are constantly thinking about the next city, you will miss the countryside along the way, and that can mean you are missing a lot of wonderful scenery.

However, you might ask the question, 'How can I live a fulfilling life right now, while still building for the future?' The answer is that you do not have to choose either now or the future ('either/or'), you can actually address both ('and both')! That is, we can be mindful of today and take time to make plans for the future. Sometimes as therapists we are invited to work with just one type of approach and some would go so far as to say that a particular approach is the only way. Our experience tells us that we can apply 'and both' to our work, and this is what we have done in this book.

Hopefully, through taking a holistic and multimodal approach, you have learnt a number of useful ways to manage the stress and anxiety. We certainly believe the skills you have learnt will generalise to other challenges in your life and will be helping you long after your original stress and anxiety problems have gone. Thank you for the opportunity to share our ideas with you, and all the best for the next phase of your journey. Bon voyage!

TRAVEL DIARY

FURTHER
RESOURCES

Books

Aisbett, B. 1993, *Living with It: A survivor's guide to panic attacks*, Angus & Robertson, Sydney.

Aisbett, B. 2008, *Book of It: 10 steps to conquering anxiety*, HarperCollins Publishers, Sydney.

Arden, J. 2009, *The Heal Your Anxiety Workbook: New techniques for moving from panic to inner peace*, Fair Winds Press, USA.

Fox, B. 1996, *Power Over Panic: Freedom from panic/anxiety related disorders*, Longman, Australia.

Freeston, M. and Meares, K. 2008, *Overcoming Worry: A Self-Help Guide Using Cognitive Behavioural Techniques*, Robinson, London.

Gilbert, P. 2009, *The Compassionate Mind*, Constable, London.

Gilbert, P. 2009, *Overcoming Depression: A Self-Help Guide Using Cognitive Behavioural Techniques* (3rd edition), Robinson, London.

Greenberger, D. & Padesky, C. 1995, *Mind Over Mood: Change how you feel by changing the way you think*, The Guilford Press, New York.

Harris, R. 2008, *The Happiness Trap*, Robinson, London.

Harris, R. 2009, *ACT made simple: An easy-to-read primer on acceptance and commitment therapy*, New Harbinger Publications, United States of America.

Harris, R. 2011, *The Confidence Gap*, Robinson, London.

Hassed, C. 2002, *Know Thyself: The stress release programme*, Michelle Anderson Publishing, Melbourne.

Hopkins, C. 1997, *101 shortcuts to relaxation*, Bloomsbury, London.

Howell, C. 2009, *Keeping the Blues Away: The ten-step guide to reducing the relapse of depression*, Radcliffe Publishing, Oxford.

Johnstone, M. 2007, *I Had A Black Dog*, Robinson, London.

Kennerley, H. 1997, *Overcoming Anxiety: A Self-Help Guide Using Cognitive Behavioural Techniques*, Robinson, London.

Kidman, A. 1998, *Feeling Better: A guide to mood management*, Biochemical and General Services, Sydney.

Lewis, D. 2004, *Free your Breath, Free your Life: How conscious breathing can relieve stress, increase vitality and help you live more fully*, Shambhala Publications, Boston.

Marks, I. 1978, *Living with Fear: Understanding and coping with anxiety*, McGraw-Hill, Berkshire, England.

Mischie, D. 2008, *Hurry Up and Meditate*, Allen & Unwin, Sydney.

Morgan, A. 2000, *What is Narrative Therapy?*, Dulwich Centre Publications, Adelaide.

Tanner, S. and Ball, J. 1991, *Beating the Blues: A self-help approach to overcoming depression*, Doubleday, Sydney.

Tirch, D. 2012, *The Compassionate Mind Approach to Overcoming Anxiety*, Robinson, London.

Wells, A. 1997, *Cognitive Therapy of Anxiety Disorders: A practice manual and conceptual guide*, John Wiley and Sons, New York.

Wilson, P. 1995, *Instant Calm*, Penguin, Melbourne.

Wilson, P. 2005, *Perfect Balance: Create time and space for all parts of your life*, Penguin Books, Melbourne.

Wilson Schaef, A. 2000, *Meditations for Living in Balance: Daily solutions for people who do too much*, HarperCollins, New York.

Relaxation CDs

'Keeping the blues away', programme including general relaxation CD. Available from: http://www.radcliffe-oxford.com/books/bookdetail. aspx?ISBN=1846193729

'Letting go of stress and anxiety', relaxation CD by Dr Cate Howell and Dr Michele Murphy. Available from: http://www.cooindacreations.com

Mindfulness CDs by Russ Harris. Available from: http://www.actmindfully. com.au/cds_and_books

Websites

British Psychological Society (BPS): www.bps.org.uk

British Society of Clinical Hypnosis: www.bsch.org.uk

SANE UK (Information about mental illness): www.sane.org.uk

British Association for Behavioural and Cognitive Psychotherapies (BABCP) (information about how to find a CBT therapist): www.babcp.co.uk

Mind (information about mental health): www.mind.org.uk

Rethink (advice and support about mental health): www.rethink.org

British Association for Counselling & Psychotherapy (BACP) (information on how to find a counsellor or psychotherapist): www.bacp.org.uk

Websites for young people

Young Minds (mental health and wellbeing): www.youngminds.org.uk

BIBLIOGRAPHY

American Psychiatric Association, 2004, *Diagnostic and Statistical Manual of Mental Disorders (DSM-IV-TR)*, American Psychiatric Association, Washington.

Arden, J. 2009, *The Heal Your Anxiety Workbook: New techniques for moving from panic to inner peace*, Fair Winds Press, USA.

Beck, A. 1990, *Cognitive Therapy and Emotional Disorders*, Blackwell Scientific Publications, London.

Brasier, D. 1997, *Zen Therapy: Transcending the sorrows of the human mind*, Wiley and Sons, New York.

Burns, D.D. 1980, *Feeling Good: The new mood therapy, Information Australia Group*, Sydney.

Burns, R. 1992, *10 skills for working with stress*, Business and Professional Publishers, Sydney.

Corey, G. 1977, *Theory and Practice of Counselling and Psychotherapy*, Brookes/Cole, Monterey, USA.

Freeman, L. 2009, *Mosby's Complementary and Alternative Medicine: A research-based approach*, 3rd edition, Mosby Elsevier, St Louis, USA.

Forsyth, J. and Eifert, G. 2007, *The Mindfulness and Acceptance Workbook for Anxiety*, New Harbinger Publications, Oakland, USA.

Greenberger, D. and Padesky, C. 1995, *Mind over Mood: Change how you feel by changing the way you think*, The Guildford Press, New York.

Harris, R. 2007, *The Happiness Trap: Stop struggling, start living*, Exisle Publishing, Wollombi, NSW.

Harris, R. 2009, *ACT made simple: An easy-to-read primer on Acceptance and Commitment Therapy*, New Harbinger Publications, Oakland, USA.

Hayes, S.C., Strosahl, K. D. and Wilson, K.G. 2003, *Acceptance and Commitment Therapy: An experiential approach to behaviour change*, Guilford Press, New York.

Howell, C. 2009, *Keeping the Blues Away: The ten-step guide to reducing the relapse of depression*, Radcliffe Publishing, Oxford, UK.

Hunter, M. 1988, *Daydreams for Discovery. A manual for hypnotherapists*, Sea Walk Press, West Vancouver.

Jeffers, S. 1987, *Feel the Fear and Do it Anyway: How to turn your fear and indecision into confidence and action*, Vermilion, London.

Launer, J. 2002, *Narrative-based Primary Care: A practical guide*, Radcliffe Medical Press, Abingdon, Oxford, UK.

Marks, I. 1978, *Living with Fear: Understanding and coping with anxiety*, McGraw-Hill, London.

McKeith, G. 2004, *The Plan That Will Change Your Life: You are what you eat*, Penguin, Melbourne.

O'Connor, R. 2001, *Active Treatment of Depression*, Norton, New York.

Page, A. and Page, C. 1996, *Assert Yourself! How to resolve conflict and say what you mean without being passive or aggressive*, Gore & Osment, Sydney.

Reynolds, D. 2002, *A Handbook for Constructive Living*, University of Hawai'i Press, Honolulu.

Wells, A. 1997, *Cognitive Therapy of Anxiety Disorders: A practice manual and conceptual guide*, John Wiley and Sons, New York.

White, C. and Denborough, D. 1998, *Introducing Narrative Therapy: A collection of practice-based writings*, Dulwich Centre Publications, Adelaide.

World Health Organization Collaborating Centre, 2004, *Management of Mental Disorders*, 4th edition, vol. 1, World Health Organization Collaborating Centre for Evidence in Mental Health Policy, Darlinghurst, NSW.

ENDNOTES

INTRODUCTION
1. Harris, R. 2007, *The Happiness Trap: Stop struggling, start living*, Exisle Publishing, Wollombi, NSW, p. 16.

CHAPTER 1
1. Yerkes, R.M. and Dodson, J.D. 1908, 'The relation of strength of stimulus to rapidity of habit-formation', Journal of Comparative Neurology and Psychology, vol. 18, p. 459.

2. Siegel, D.J. 2007, *The Mindful Brain: Reflection and attunement in the cultivation of wellbeing*, Norton & Company, New York City, p. 30.

3. Arden, J. 2009, *The Heal Your Anxiety Workbook: New techniques for moving from panic to inner peace*, Fair Winds Press, USA, p. 41.

4. McNeilly, R. 1996, 'Individualising stress and the benefits of hypnosis', *Australian Family Physician*, vol. 25, p. 1261.

5. Forsyth, J. and Eifert, G. 2007, *The Mindfulness and Acceptance Workbook for Anxiety*, New Harbinger Publications, Oakland, USA, p. 30.

6. ibid.

7. Edelman, S. 2002, *Change Your Thinking*, 2nd edition, ABC Books, Sydney, p. 102.

8. Andrews, G., et al. 2003, *The Treatment of Anxiety Disorders: Clinician guides and patient manuals*, Cambridge University Press, Melbourne, p. 26.

9. Somers, J., et al. 2006, 'Prevalence and incidence studies of anxiety disorders: A systematic review of the literature', *Canadian Journal of Psychiatry*, vol. 51, no. 2, p. 100.

10. Australian Institute of Health and Welfare, 2007, *Incidence and Prevalence of Chronic Diseases*, AIHW, Canberra.

11. Somers, J., et al. loc. cit.

12. Hendricks, G., et al. 2008, 'Cognitive-behavioural therapy for late-life anxiety disorders: A systematic review and meta-analysis', *Acta Psychiatr Scand*, vol. 117, p. 403.

13. Reid, W. and Wise, M. 1995, *DSM-IV Training Guide*, Brunner/Mazel Publishers, New York, p. 146.

14. Arden, J. 2009, op. cit., p. 24.

15. Beck, A. and Emery, G. 1985, *Anxiety Disorders and Phobias: A cognitive perspective*, Basic Books, p. 15.

16. Forsyth, J. and Eifert, G. op. cit., p. 48.

17. Evans, B., Coman, G. and Burrows, G. D. 1998, *Your Guide to Understanding and Managing Stress*, Mental Health Foundation of Australia, Victoria.

18. Arden, J. op. cit., p. 18.

19. World Health Organization Collaborating Centre, 2004, *Management of Mental Disorders*, 4th edition, vol. 1. World Health Organization Collaborating Centre for Evidence in Mental Health Policy, Darlinghurst, NSW, p. 243.

20. Andrews, G. et al., op. cit., p. 202.

21. Beck, A. and Emery, G. op. cit., p. 83.

22. Howell, C. 2009, *Keeping the Blues Away: The ten-step guide to reducing the relapse of depression*, Radcliffe, Oxford, p. 19.

23. World Health Organization Collaborating Centre, op. cit., p. 211.

24. Hendricks, G., et al. op. cit., p. 403.

25. Andrews, G., et al. op. cit., p. 366.

26. Wells, A. 1997, *Cognitive Therapy of Anxiety Disorders: A practice manual and conceptual guide*, John Wiley and Sons, New York, p. 110.

27. ibid., p. 122.

28. Howell, C. op. cit., p. 52.

29. Reynolds, D. 2002, *A Handbook for Constructive Living*, University of Hawai'i Press, Honolulu, p. 55.

CHAPTER 2

1. NASA. 2009, 'One small step', retrieved 24 January 2010: http://history.nasa.gov/alsj/a11/a11.step.html

2. Miller, W.R. and Rollnick, S. 2002, *Motivational Interviewing: Preparing people for change*, 2nd edition, Guilford Press, New York, p. 8.

3. Kidman, A. 1986, *Tactics for Change: A self-help manual*. Biochemical and General Services, Sydney, p. 14.

4. Harris, R. 2009, *ACT Made Simple: An easy-to-read primer on Acceptance and Commitment Therapy*, New Harbinger Publications, Oakland, USA, p. 11.

5. Harris, R. 2007, op. cit., p. 296.

6. ibid., p. 211.

7. ibid.

8. Howell, C. op. cit., p. 23.

9. Edelman, S. 2002, *Change Your Thinking*, 2nd edition, ABC Books, Sydney, p. 291.

10. Hubbard, E. 1927, *The Note Book of Elbert Hubbard: Mottoes, epigrams, short essays, orphic sayings, and preachments*, W.H. Wise & Co.

11. Howell, C. op. cit., p. 80.

12. Lazarus, A. 2000, 'Multimodal Therapy', *Current Psychotherapies*, Corsini R.J. and Wedding, D. (eds), Brooks/Cole, Belmont, CA, p. 342.

13. Dryden, W. and Mytton, J. 1999, *Four Approaches to Counselling and Psychotherapy*, Routledge, London, p. 135.

14. Noonan, W.C. and Moyers, T.B. 1997, 'Motivational interviewing', *Journal of Substance Use*, vol. 2, no. 1, p. 8.

15. ibid., p. 9.

16. ibid.

17. Miller, W.R. and Rollnick, S. op. cit., p. 8.

18. Wells, A. op. cit., p. 1.

19. Dryden, W. and Mytton, J. op. cit., p. 12.

20. Kidman, A. 1986, op. cit., p. 28.

21. Blackburn, I. and Davidson, K. 1990, *Cognitive Therapy for Depression and Anxiety: A practical guide*, Blackwell Scientific Publications, Oxford, p. 50.

22. Beck, A. and Weishaar, M. 2000, 'Cognitive Therapy', *Current Psychotherapies*, Corsini R. and Wedding, D. op. cit., p. 243.

23. ibid.

24. Edelman, S. op. cit., p. 2.

25. White, M. 1991, 'Deconstruction and therapy'. *Dulwich Centre Newsletter*, vol. 3, pp. 36–8.

26. Siegel, D.J. op. cit., pp. 10, 17.

27. ibid., p. 31.

28. Reynolds, D. op. cit., p. 4.

29. ibid., p. 21.

30. Harris, R. 2007, op. cit., p. 60.

31. Harris, R. 2009, op. cit., p. 110.

32. Howell, C. op. cit., p. 11.

33. ibid., p. 41.

34. Kinrys, G., Coleman, E. and Rothstein, E. 2009, 'Natural remedies for anxiety disorders: Potential use and clinical applications', *Depression and Anxiety*, vol. 26, p. 260.

35. Ernst, E., Rand, J.I. and Stevinson, C. 1998, 'Complementary therapies for depression. An overview', *Archives of General Psychiatry*, vol. 55, p. 1026.

36. Wilson, P. 1995, *Instant Calm*, Penguin, Ringwood, Victoria, p. 56.

37. World Health Organization Collaborating Centre, op. cit., p. 272.

38. Howell, C. op. cit., p. 54.

39. Hassed, C. 2002, *Know Thyself: The stress release program*, Michelle Anderson Publishing, Melbourne, p. 50.

40. O'Donoghue, M. 2009, 'Teaching meditation 1: concentration on the breath', *Journal of the Australian and New Zealand Student Services Association*, vol. 33, p. 62.

CHAPTER 3

1. Benson, H. 1977, *The Relaxation Response*, Collins, Fountain Books, UK.

2. Harris, R. 2009, op. cit., p. 8.

3. Harris, R. 2007, op. cit., p. 164.

4. Wilson, P. 2005, *Perfect Balance: Create time and space for all parts of your life*, Penguin, Melbourne, p. 25.

5. Selye, H. 1978, *The Stress of Life*, (revised edition), McGraw-Hill Book Co, New York, p. 36.

6. Yerkes, R.M. and Dodson, J.D. op. cit., pp. 459–82.

7. Wilson, P. 2005, op. cit., p. 55.

8. Burns, A.M. and Dunlop, R.K. 2001, 'Which basket are your eggs in?': Emotional investments from early adolescence to early adulthood among sons and daughters of divorced and non-divorced parents'. *Journal of Family Studies*, vol. 7, no. 1, p. 56.

9. Wilson, P. 2005, op. cit., p. 198.

10. NHMRC. 2003, *Dietary Guidelines for Australian Adults*, Commonwealth of Australia, Canberra.

11. Osiecki, H. 2006, *The Nutrient Bible*, 7th edition, Bio Concepts Publishing, Queensland, p. 141.

12. Beim, M. 1993, *Beaming with Health: The simple guide to feeling good*, ABC Books, Sydney, p. 41.

13. Cooper, R., Morre, J. and Morre, D. 2005, 'Medicinal benefits of green tea: Part I. Review of non-cancer health benefits', *Journal of Alternative and Complementary Medicine*, vol. 11, no. 3, p. 521.

14. Stamford, B. 1995, 'The role of exercise in fighting depression', *The Physician and Sportsmedicine*, vol. 23, p. 79.

15. Hunter, M. 1988, *Daydreams for Discovery. A manual for hypnotherapists*, Sea Walk Press, West Vancouver, p. 69.

CHAPTER 4

1. Morgan, A. op. cit., p. 17.
2. Leonardo, E.D. and Hen, R. 2006, *Genetics of Affective and Anxiety Disorders*, Annual Review of Psychology, 57: p. 117.
3. Harris, R. 2007, 21.
4. Forsyth, J. and Eifert, G. op. cit., p. 61.
5. Howell, C. op. cit., p. 64.
6. Kidman, A. 1988, *From Thought to Action: A self-help manual*, Biochemical and General Services, Sydney, p. 13.
7. Harris, R. 2007, op. cit., p. 13.
8. ibid., p. 14.
9. ibid.
10. ibid., p. 15.
11. Forsyth, J. and Eifert, G. op. cit., p. 62.
12. Edelman, S. op. cit., p. 26.
13. Arden, J. op. cit., p. 107.
14. Howell, C. op. cit., p. 73.
15. ibid., p. 74.
16. ibid.
17. ibid., p. 77.
18. Reynolds, D. op. cit., p. 21.

CHAPTER 5

1. Wells, A. op. cit., p. 19.
2. Forsyth, J. and Eifert, G. op. cit., p. 52.
3. Wells, A. op. cit., p. 63.
4. Centre for Clinical Interventions, 2008, 'Overcoming Procrastination' module: http://www.cci.health.wa.gov.au/resources/infopax.cfm?Info_ID=50

5. ibid.

6. World Health Organization Collaborating Centre, op. cit., p. 26.

7. Andrews, G. and Hunt, C. 1998, 'Treatments that work in anxiety disorders', *Mental Health*, N.A. Keks and G.D. Burrows (eds), Australasian Medical Publishing Company Limited, Sydney, p. 26.

8. Howell, C. op. cit., p. 46.

9. ibid., p. 110.

10. Bolton, R. 1987, *People Skills: How to assert yourself, listen to others, and resolve conflicts*, Simon & Schuster, New York, p. 123.

11. Williams, C. 2000, *Being Assertive: A five areas approach*, University of Leeds Innovations, p. 2.

12. Howell, C. loc. cit.

CHAPTER 6

1. Reynolds, D. op. cit., p. 21.

2. Harris, R. 2009, op. cit., p. 2.

3. Forsyth, J. and Eifert, G. op. cit., p. 16.

4. ibid., p. 45.

5. Harris, R. 2009, op. cit., p. 10.

6. Harris, R. 2007, op. cit., p. 108.

7. Harris, R. 2009, op. cit., p. 9.

8. ibid., p. 97.

9. ibid., p. 9.

10. Harris, R. 2007, op. cit., p. 195.

11. Hilgard, F. 1977, *Divided Consciousness: Multiple controls on human thought and action*, John Wiley and Sons, New York.

12. Harris, R. 2009, op. cit., p. 11.

13. ibid., p. 210.

14. Harris, R. 2007, op. cit., p. 53.

15. Forsyth, J. and Eifert, G. op. cit., p. 242.

16. Harris, R. 2009, op. cit., p. 137.

17. Forsyth, J. and Eifert, G. op. cit., p. 132.

18. ibid.

19. ibid., p. 76.

20. ibid., p. 138.

21. ibid., p. 240.

22. Kelly, P. 2000, '*Malcolm Fraser*', *Australian Prime Minister*, M. Grattan (ed), Holland Publishers, Sydney.

23. Shaw, G.B. 1947, *Back to Methuselah*, Oxford University Press, Oxford.

CHAPTER 7

1. Morgan, A. op. cit., p. 5.

2. ibid., p. 13.

3. ibid., p. 14.

4. Harris, R. 2007, op. cit., p. 187.

5. White, M. 1991, '*Deconstruction and therapy*', Dulwich Centre Newsletter, vol 3, p. 29.

6. Harris, R. 2007, loc. cit.

7. ibid., p. 188.

8. Morgan, A. op. cit., p. 10.

9. ibid., p. 9.

10. Robertson, F. and Schubert, L. 1997, 'Standing up to the messages of stress', *Journal of Deconstruction and Narrative Ideas in Therapeutic Practice*, vol. 2, p. 33.

11. White, M. and Epston, D. 1990, *Literate Means to Therapeutic Ends*, Dulwich Centre Publications, Adelaide, p. 83.

12. Monk, G. 1997, '*How narrative therapy works*', *Narrative Therapy in Practice: The archaeology of hope.*, G. Monk, et al., (eds), Jossey Bass Publishers, San Francisco, CA, p. 27.

13. Freedman, J. & Combs, G. 1993, *Narrative Therapy: The social construction of preferred realities*, Norton, New York, p. 117.

14. Linell, S. and Cora, D. 1993, *Discoveries: A group resource guide for women who have been sexually abused in childhood*, Dympna House Publications, Sydney, p. 21.

15. Dodding, C.J., et al. 2008, 'All in for mental health: A pilot study of group therapy for people experiencing anxiety and/or depression and a significant other of their choice', *Mental Health in Family Medicine*, vol. 5 p. 41.

16. Mitchell, J., et al. 2005, 'Computer-assisted group therapy for the treatment of depression and anxiety in general practice', *Primary Care Mental Health*, vol. 3, p. 28.

17. Morgan, A. op. cit., p. 13.

18. ibid., p. 17.

19. ibid., p. 68.

20. ibid., p. 53.

21. Murphy, M.1997, 'Humorous stories: Antidote to despair? A discussion of the place of humour in therapy', *Journal of Deconstruction and Narrative Ideas in Therapeutic Practice*, vol. 2, p. 9.

22. Morgan, A. op. cit., p. 15.

23. Sykes-Wylie, M. 1994, *Panning for Gold*, The Networker, Nov–Dec.

24. Morgan, A. op. cit., p. 68.

25. ibid., p. 14.

26. ibid., p. 59.

27. Robertson, F. & Schubert, L. op. cit., p. 37.

28. Morgan, A. op. cit., p. 79.

29. ibid., p. 78.

30. Murphy, M. 1998, 'Training as co-research', *Narratives of Therapists' Lives*, M. White, Editor. Dulwich Centre Publications, Adelaide, p. 181.

31. Morgan, A. op. cit., p. 84.

CHAPTER 8

1. Harris, R. 2007, op. cit., p. 71.

2. Reynolds, D. op. cit., p. 77.

3. Harris, R. 2007, loc. cit.

4. ibid., p. 73.

5. ibid., p. 71.

6. Forsyth, J. and Eifert, G. op. cit., p. 13.

7. ibid., p. 52.

8. ibid., p. 55.

9. ibid., p. 190.

10. Gazal, C. 2004, *The Happy Toddler*, Insight Publications, Melbourne, p. 117.

11. Forsyth, J. and Eifert, G. op. cit., p. 302.

12. Harris, R. 2009, op. cit., p. 25.

13. Harris, R. 2007, op. cit., p. 77.

14. Reynolds, D. op. cit., p. 172.

15. Harris, R. 2007, op. cit., p. 188.

16. ibid., p. 181.

17. ibid., p. 185.

18. Edelman, S. op. cit., p. 149.

19. Reynolds, D. op. cit., p. 76.

20. ibid., p. 77.

21. Howell, C. op. cit., p. 82.

22. Harris, R. 2007, op. cit., p. 77.

23. ibid., p. 72.

24. Neff, K. 2003, *'Self compassion: An alternative conceptualisation of a healthy attitude toward oneself'*, Self and Identity, vol. 2, p. 86.

25. ibid., p. 88.

26. Forsyth, J. and Eifert, G. op. cit., p. 206.

27. ibid.

28. ibid., p. 205.

29. Neff, K. op. cit., p. 90.

30. Forsyth, J. and Eifert, G. op. cit., p. 210.

31. Kornfield, J. 1994, *Buddha's Little Instruction Book*, Random House, New York.

CHAPTER 9

1. Wells, A. op. cit., p. 26.

2. Forsyth, J. and Eifert, G. op. cit., p. 45.

3. World Health Organization Collaborating Centre, op. cit., p. 273.

4. Howell, C. op. cit., p. 60.

5. ibid., p. 68.

6. Andrews, G., et al. op. cit., p. 270.

7. ibid., p. 366.

8. ibid.

9. World Health Organization Collaborating Centre, op. cit., p. 251.

10. Australian Centres for Posttraumatic Mental Health 2007, *Australian Guidelines for the Treatment of Adults with Acute Stress Disorder and Posttraumatic Stress Disorder*, ACPMH, Melbourne, p. 28.

CHAPTER 10

1. Morgan, A. op. cit., p. 111.

2. Howell, C. op. cit., p. 120.

3. Williams, C. op. cit., p. 2.

4. Kupfer, D.J. 1991, '*Long-term treatment of depression*', Journal of Clinical Psychiatry, vol. 52 (supplement), p. 28.

5. Howell, C. loc. cit.

6. Williams, C. loc. cit.

7. Forsyth, J. and Eifert, G. op. cit., p. 260.

8. Reynolds, D. op. cit., p. 61.

INDEX